PLANS OF ARCHITECTURE

"Most of the beauty in San Diego is yet to come," we said in 1962.

May this book help you to create beauty in the city in your own way, and according to the best ideas of your era. Please make a wide search for good design ideas.

Best wishes for a handsome community in the next century.

Lloyd Ruocco AIA

Ilse Hamann Ruocco

RESTAURANT DETAILS

WITHDRAWN

Author

Francisco Asensio Cerver

Editorial director

Jordi Vigué

Project co-ordinator

Ivan Bercedo (architect)

Layout

Estudi Bosch, S.L.

Translation

Harry Paul Carey

Proofreading

David Buss

Photographs

Robert Lam *(La Placita)*; Mario Pignata-Monti (Gagnaire); Viviane Vives *(Chango's)*; Felix von Schlenburg *(Daphne)*; Antoine Bootz *(89)*;
Elliot Kaufman *(Caroline's)*; Chris Gascoigne/VIEW *(Oxo Tower)*; Dub Rogers *(Grille 5115)*; Tuca Reinés *(Cantaloup)*; Paul Warchol *(Nobu, Payard, Mohegan)*

1998 ⊛ Francisco Asensio Cerver   ISBN: 0-8230-7186-3   Printed in Spain

Whitney Library of Design
an imprint of Watson and Guptill Publication/New York
1515 Broadway
New York-NY 10036 USA

As time goes by, designing leisure spaces is becoming an increasingly independent field within interior design and architecture. In particular, when a designer is commissioned a restaurant he or she has to take on a double challenge: on one hand they have to fit out an eating place, while at the same time creating an attractive atmosphere which seduces people into entering. Half way between architecture, graphic design, scenography, furniture design, interiorism and gastronomy, the building of a restaurant has become a melting pot of activities.

Rarely elsewhere are the details so important as they are in these type of establishments. The restaurant is a land of subtleties. Just as when you prepare a dish the small things end up giving it character the aroma, the sauce, the layout on the plate, in the same way in the design of a restaurant every feature must be studied and carefully weighed up: the lighting, the acoustics, the form of the bar, the position of the rest rooms, the dinner service, the menu card and the floor.

In the following pages our aim has been to present different types of restaurants, right through from the restaurant created by one of the most famous chefs in the world to a small eating house measuring 24x24x24 ft., designed to be fitted in anywhere, in Iquique Park, 1,200 m from Santiago, Chile. There are Japanese restaurants, and Mexican, premises which overlook the Thames and the dome of Saint Paul's cathedral (Oxo Tower), or restaurants that are in a basement (Caroline`s Comedy Club).

Different circumstances in every case mean that the project strategy has to be distinct. It is interesting to observe how these differences affect the drawing, the plans, and all in all, the tools of the designer. To illustrate this, one need only compare the drawings of the Mohegan Sun Casino to those of the Oxo Tower, or those of La Placita with those of the 89, to realize that it is not only the aspirations of the designer that count but also the type of restaurant, the food offered and the public at which it is aimed.

Therefore, in every place certain features become more important than others, depending on the character of the restaurant. In La Placita we can observe how the lamps have been elaborated as if they were the work of a goldsmith. In Chango's, it is the covering of the building and the dramatic natural light that have received the most attention. In Caroline`s Comedy Club, the chromatic patterns of all the features, the graphic design and the artificial lighting give the project its identity. The modules of the Zoficentros are constructed almost as if they were furniture. All these observations demonstrate that the projects can not be analyzed from the same perspective. Just looking at a few photos is not enough to understand the internal process of each proposal.

We believe that detailed analysis is the most objective way of comprehending each project. Parallelly, the opportunity to study how the details of very distinct project have been constructed convert the following pages into a catalogue of useful solutions for any professional dedicated to leisure architecture. We are used to publications showing us the projects without going into how they were done. In this book we rectify that error.

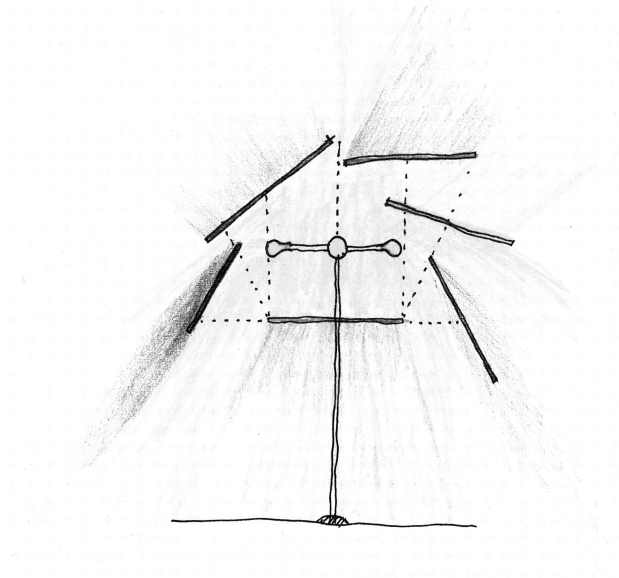

La Placita

Stephen Lombardi

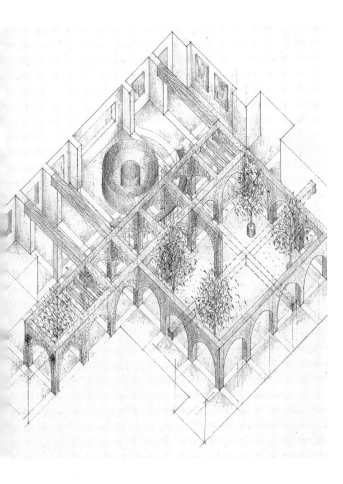

Axonometry.

Location: *Times Square, Causeway Bay, Hong Kong.*
Design: *Stephen Lombardi.*
Year of opening: *1995.*
Project director: *CYS, Winnie Lee.*
Building contractor: *Kuen Lee Decoration Co. Ltd.*
Surface area: *7.800 square feet (725 m squared).*

La Placita is a mexican restaurant located on the thirteenth floor of a building in Times Square, Hong Kong. The aim of its promoter, Heinz Grabner, and of its designer, Stephen Lombardi, an architect from San Diego well versed in Hispanic culture, was to transfer a corner of a traditional Mexican city to the centre of the ex-British colony. In fact, the greater part of the construction and decoration materials used were literally imported from Mexico, or, as in the case of the pavement, from Los Angeles, California.

The entry into the restaurant is made through "The door of life", which is decorated with eight symbols that represent health, peace, and happiness. Inside, a corridor between two lines of arches leads from the entry to a semicircular tile covered fountain. The corridor separates the bar (with a great semicircular bar) from the restaurant.

The main room of the restaurant is a typical little village square (in Spanish "placita"): a rectangular space surrounded by arches and a porch around the edges, like in the squares of the Mexican towns and ranches. The arches are covered in wood, and the walls have been ornamented with intensely coloured stucco. Across the ceiling of the room, four enormous exposed beams run, and thus hide the lighting and air conditioning installations.

In the restaurant there are many objects which have been brought directly from Mexico. For example, the chairs are the typical seats of wood and wicker. There are also articles of precolombian origin from the Aztec or Maya cultures. However, as Stephen Lombardi has confessed, his intention was not to reproduce a Mexican town on a floor of a Hong Kong skyscraper, but rather to realize an interpretation of that culture. Therefore, the doors and the lamps have been designed by the architect himself, mixing modernity and tradition.

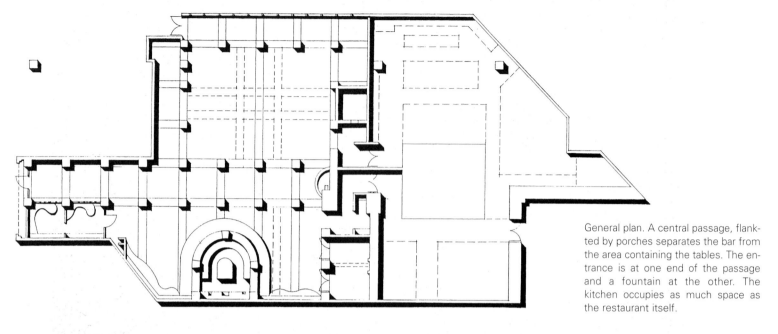

General plan. A central passage, flanked by porches separates the bar from the area containing the tables. The entrance is at one end of the passage and a fountain at the other. The kitchen occupies as much space as the restaurant itself.

On the opposite page, a detailed photo of the fountain inspired by Mexican ranches.

Below, a perspective created by a computer, in which not only have the distribution and image of the restaurant been studied, but also the materials and the colors.

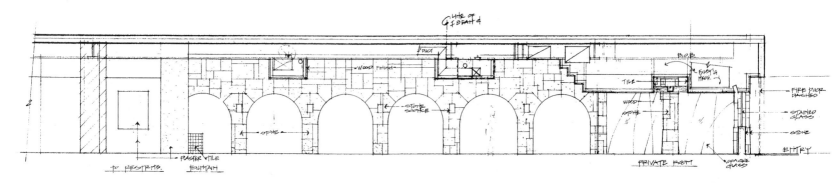

Cross section of the restaurant. The enormous wooden beams hide the air conditioning ducts.

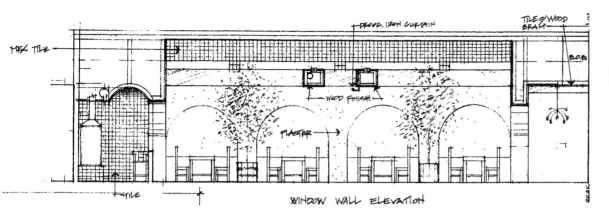

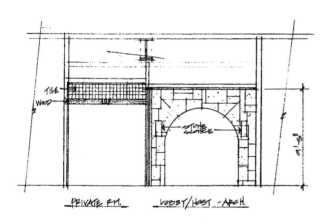

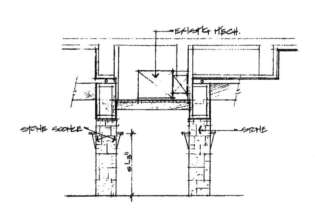

Using false ceilings of different heights, including arches and vaults, has converted this storey of the skyscraper into a tagteful and attractive space. To achieve this, the work on the different sections has been more important than developing the layout.

WINDOW WALL ELEVATION

PRIVATE RM.   LOBBY/HOST - ARCH.

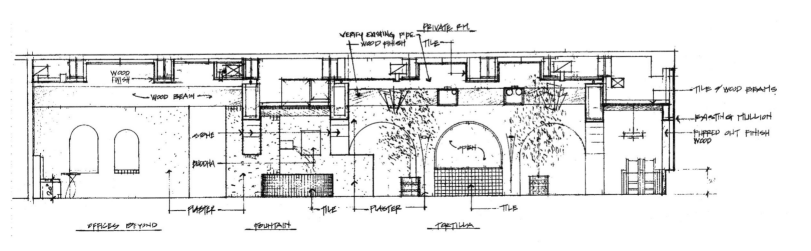

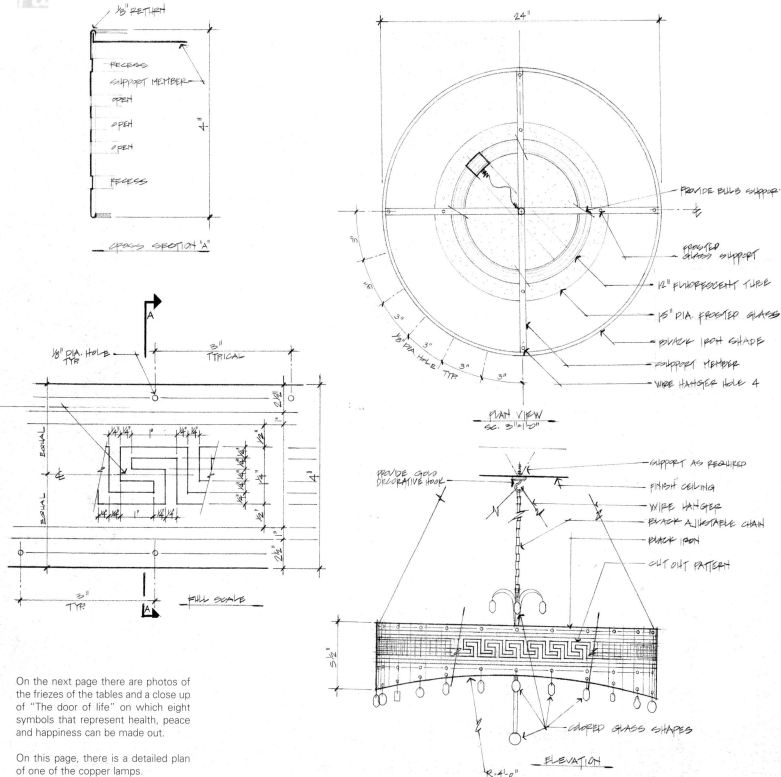

On the next page there are photos of the friezes of the tables and a close up of "The door of life" on which eight symbols that represent health, peace and happiness can be made out.

On this page, there is a detailed plan of one of the copper lamps.

Lombardi
uses traditional
iconography, but
from a modern
perspective

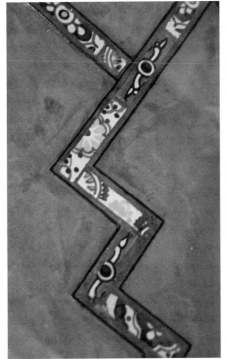

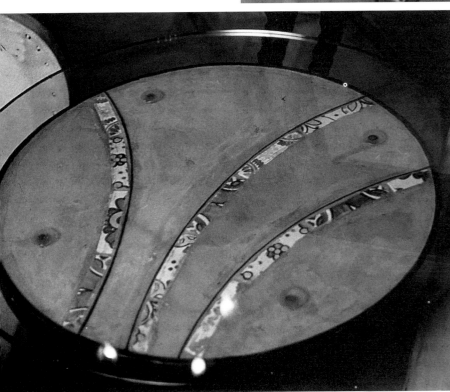

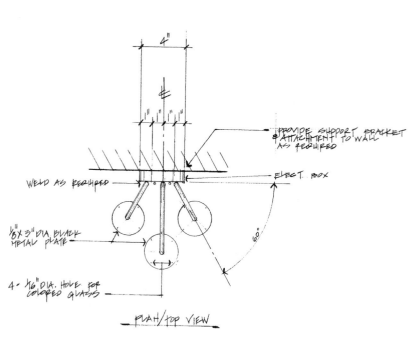

4"

PROVIDE SUPPORT BRACKET
& ATTACHMENT TO WALL
AS REQUIRED

WELD AS REQUIRED

ELECT. BOX

⅛"X 3" DIA BLACK
METAL PLATE

60°

4 - ⅟₁₆"DIA. HOLE FOR
COLORED GLASS

PLAN/TOP VIEW

⅜"BLACK METAL TUBE

BLACK METAL PLATE

4"DIA.BLACK METAL
ELECT. BOX

CANDLE SHAPE BULB

⅛"DIA BLACK IRON BENT ROD

COLORED GLASS - VARIOUS
SIZES & SHAPES

FRONT VIEW

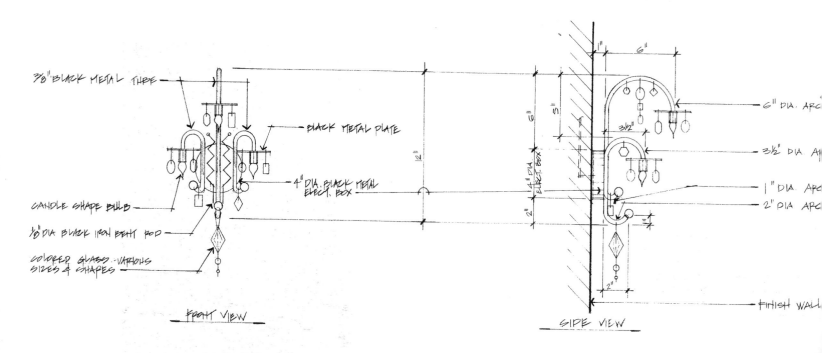

1"

6"

6"

5"

6"DIA. ARC

3½"

3½" DIA A

4" DIA
ELECT. BOX

12"

1" DIA ARC

2" DIA ARC

2"

2"

FINISH WALL

SIDE VIEW

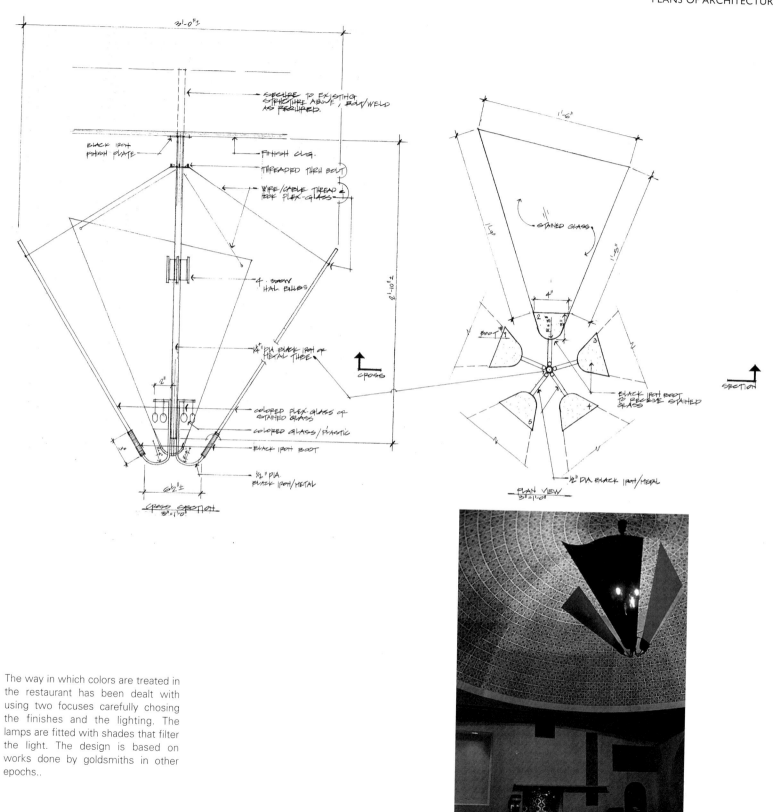

The way in which colors are treated in the restaurant has been dealt with using two focuses carefully chosing the finishes and the lighting. The lamps are fitted with shades that filter the light. The design is based on works done by goldsmiths in other epochs..

17

Gagnaire

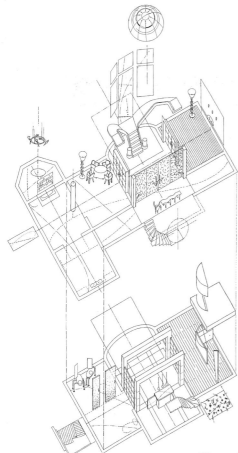

Localition: *Saint Etienne, France.*
Year of opening: *1992.*
Design: *Studio Naço (Alain Renk, Marcello Joulia).*
Collaborating architects: *Jean-François Pasqualini,*
Allard Kuyken, Beatrice Berián.
Interior designer: *Muriel Quintanilla.*
Graphic designer: *Olivier Dubos.*

The possibility of using all of the little palace gave Marcello Joulia and Alain Renk the opportunity to create a route to meander through the inside of the building, and above all around the central space near the staircase.

Pierre Gagnaire is one of the most famous chefs in the world. The restaurants in which he works are normally rated with the highly cherished three stars in the Michelin Guide, while his clients travel hundreds of kilometres to enjoy his ever changing dishes, the exotic mixture of flavors, and the aromas whipped up with a stroke of genius.

The project was born when Studio Naço was commissioned to remodel the premises that Gagnaire had been directing in Saint Etienne. However, before any work was begun, the only listed house in the city, a little palace from the nineteen thirties, was put up for sale, provoking Gagnaire into deciding to start up his own company and become an independent restaurateur.

As even Alain Renk and Marcello Joulia have confessed, working beside such a charismatic person as Pierre Gagnaire, who gives off an air of liberty, has meant that the project has gone beyond the bounds of architecture and has converted them into conductors and artistic directors of a collective, creative adventure in which painters, sculptors and photographers have participated.

The remodeling project has given equal importance to the kitchen area, the cellars and the rooms reserved for the clients. Each one of the old rooms of the small palace, or mansion, have been fitted out as a dining room. Naço have used a system of sliding doors, etched crystal screens, and grand chinese walls in varied colors to establish a play off between the differences, similarities, the union and the isolation of the different dining rooms.

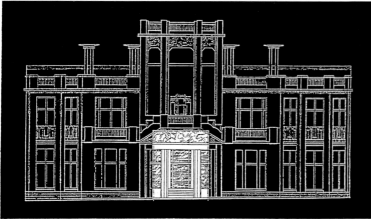

PROJET RESTAURANT PIERRE GAGNAIRE : STUDIO NAÇO.
SCULPTURE INCLUSE : FRANÇOIS SEIGNEUR.
ARCHITECTES DE LA MAISON : SUBIT ET GUYON 1930.

PHILIPPE FAVIER

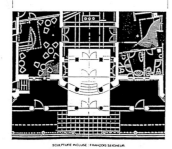

SCULPTURE INCLUSE : FRANÇOIS SEIGNEUR.

All over the restaurant the use of glass stands out.

Gagnaire set up his firm during the years when high quality cuisine was enjoying a golden period in France. Some clients traveled from afar, even coming in helicopter, to savour his choice dishes.

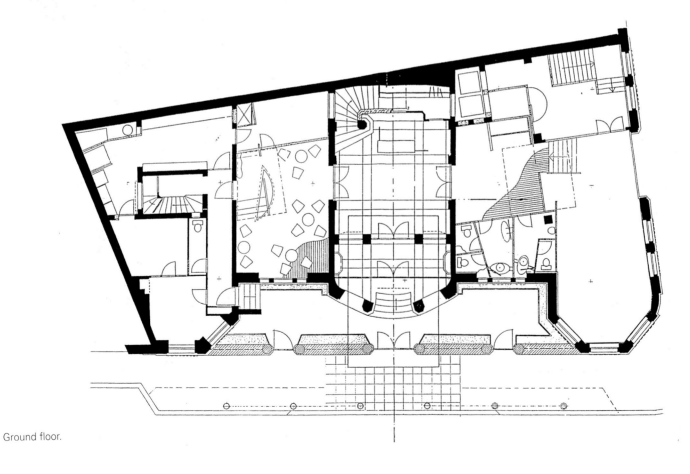

Ground floor.

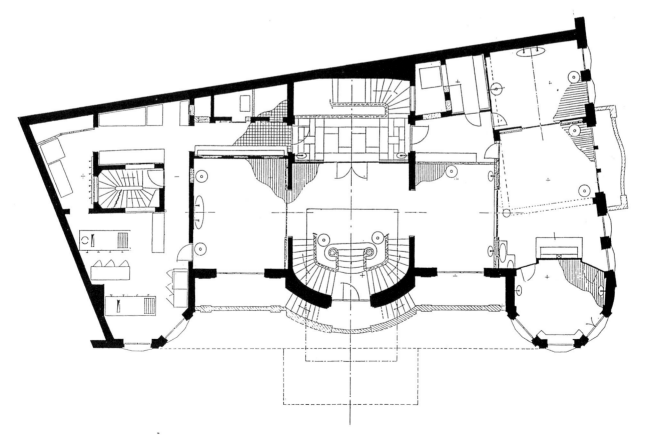

First floor.

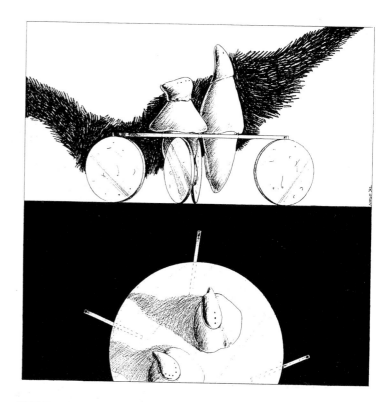

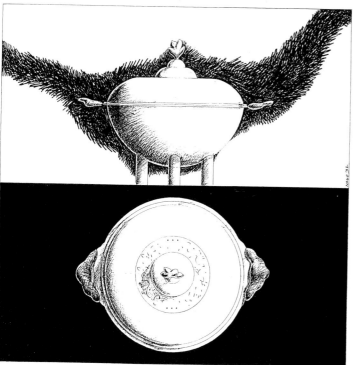

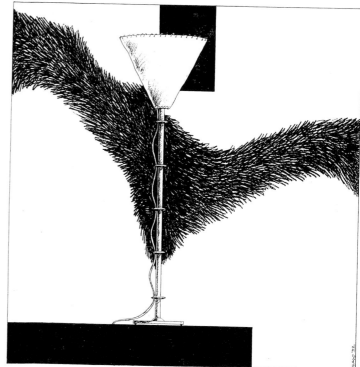

Studio Naço not only designed the architecture but also the elements of the restaurant: right through from the furniture to the cutlery, the plates and the lamps. On the previous page, you can see four examples of the ideas they came up with, and on this page, some of the results.

One of the characteristics of Gagnaire is the plastic art applied to all the surfaces, whether they be walls or glass screens. Studio Naço superimposed different layers in such a way that the same object can create different impressions. The graphic elements are in some cases signs and hieroglyphics that can enclose a mystery; in others they are simply letters or texts.

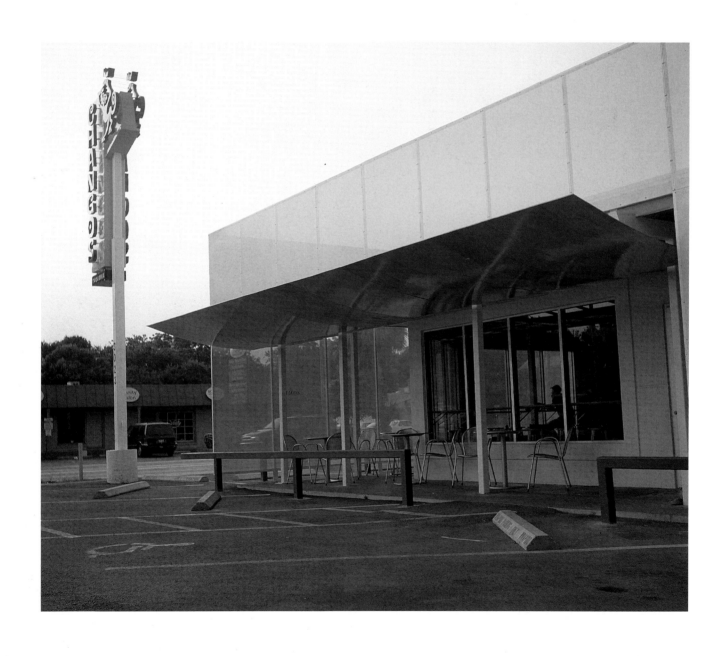

The new frame wall will create mystery while allowing a new, simpler, form to emerge – Also plays on the variation of transparencies.
the wall will also help filter some of the west sun.

wd soffits to match interior
wd. overhangs & shade for skylight

ext. overhang.

60 percent open.

23% open

Screen wall across the front

Location: *Austin, Texas, United States.*
Year of opening: *1998.*
Design: *Morris Jerome Neal, Darrell Kreitz.*

Morris Jerome Neal, an architect, and Darrell Kreitz, a cinema director, formed Pairagringo's with the intention of only designing restaurants. Both of them were to maintain their respective activities parallelly for they believe that restaurants have basically become theatrical and cinematic spaces, meaning that the work of an architect is similar to that of a set designer.

The design of Chango's has allowed them to put these ideas into practice. The task which they were to carry out was the remodeling of an existing building by incorporating metal sheets and screens, playing with the daylight and imaginatively working on the color scheme. They were to gut the building.

The exterior has been completely dressed in sheet metal, giving all the surface a homogenous look and tidying up the appearance of the old construction. According to the zones, the sheet metal is either opaque or perforated, thus playing on the variation and transparencies. Moreover, during the day the perforated sheet metal offers protection from the intense Texas sun, while at night it lets the artificial light of the interior glow out, thus advertising the presence of the restaurant in the darkness.

A skylight goes all the way across the restaurant, changing the character of the space. It is not merely a lighting element: it is used to make the interior more dynamic thanks to the shadows which it casts, especially those of the beams on the floor.

Undoubtedly, M.J. Neal and Darrel Kreitz were searching for an iconography based on the road movie. Pairagringos was created to design restaurants with a theatrical feel.

The signs and hoordings are decisively important in the "look" of the building. While the façade is altmost a single, abstract, unadorned phone-a screen, both the sign announcing the name and the hoording over the door function as visual reference points.

In this exploded axonometric view you can appreciate how the idea was to use a series of planes to play with the daylight.

In the photo below, the two designers, Morris Jerome Neal and Darrell Kreitz, appear.

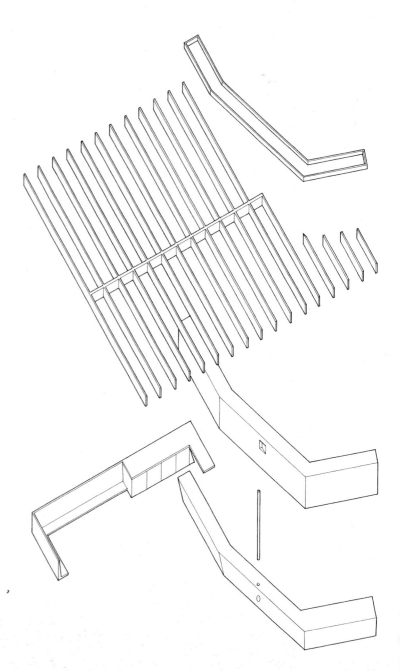

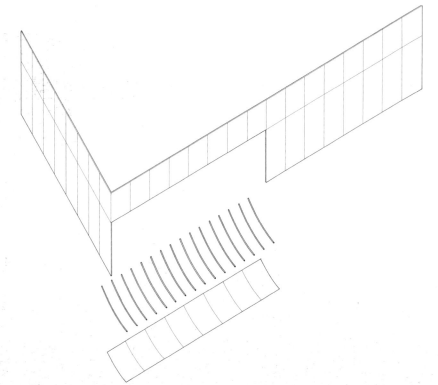

On these two pages you can appreciate the small details of the treatment given to the façade of the restaurant. The use of perforated sheet metal provokes the appearance of diffused transparencies coming through the façade. The boundary between the inside and the outside has become vaguer. Choosing mesh metal chairs has intensified this sensation.

The structure of the entrance awning is seen here from the inside. In this way the visitor can be shown the superimposed skin of the façade.

This is an axonometric view of the façade and the awning, in which the rib like strucure is discernible.

Location: *Preyscott Place, Chelsea, London.*
Design: *Michael Johnson, Laurie Bradley.*
Year of opening: *1994.*
Client: *Mogens Tholstrup.*
Contractor: *Mills Shopfitting.*
Furniture: *M.A.S. Furniture.*
Structure: *Price & Myers.*
Acoustics: *Paul Gillerion.*
Air conditioning: *Mala Engineering.*

The restaurant Daphne used to belong to a theatre actress of the same name. When Mogens Tholstrup bought it, in the middle of the nineties, he thought that the decadent and dramatic ambience of the interior would need to be refurbished.

The intention underlying all that he did was to create a decoration with an European aspect, more specifically Italian, that would be a suitable backdrop for the plates from the south of Europe which were to be the main attraction of the business. The inicial scheme was designed in tandem by Mogens Tholstrup and Michael Johnson Architects.

The first decision was to change the position of the kitchen to convert the space which it occupied previously into an indoor garden lit by a grand skylight. This room is on the upper floor, at the back of the restaurant, which means that the client, after passing through some rooms without daylight, is surprised by the discovery of an indoor garden. Moreover, the skylight can be opened electrically: half of the skylight moves sideways, coming to rest on top of the other half. During the summer, a miraculous season in London if it really does arrive, the whole skylight opens up and the room becomes a genuine outdoor garden.

They decided that the colors and the interior finishings were to have earthy tones and textures, with the aim of creating a warm atmosphere in the main part of the restaurant. Mogens Tholstrup had been inspired by the ornamentation of a portico, an arcade like structure, that he had seen in Florence, to design a Tuscan motif that was later adapted by Michael Johnson to construct the front door, the bar counter and for the pattern of the waistcoats of the waiters.

Ground floor.

First floor.

A view of the counter in the bar, located just next to the entrance and to the cloak room. The interior finishings have been chosen with the intention of creating a warm and cosy atmosphere that brings Tuscany to mind.

As the photos here show, both the bar and the waistcoat of the waiters have the same pattern. It is a drawing that the owner of the restaurant, Mogens Thostrup, saw on a portico in Florence and that Michael Johnson then adapted.

In the different sections you can see how Michael Johnson put the loft, the floors and the terrace at the back of the premises to good use.

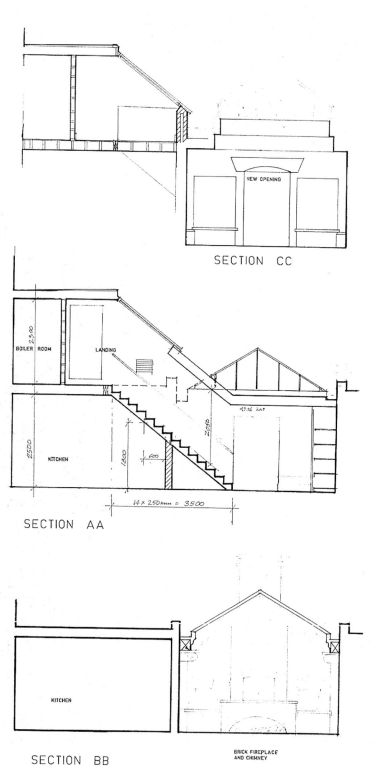

NEW OPENING

SECTION CC

2.500

BOILER ROOM

LANDING

2500

KITCHEN

1800

600

2050

14 × 250mm = 3500

SECTION AA

KITCHEN

SECTION BB

BRICK FIREPLACE AND CHIMNEY

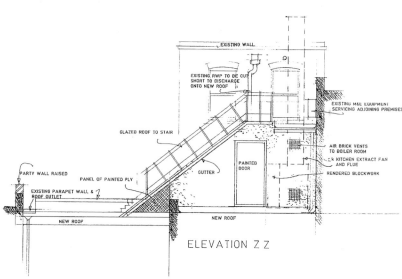

EXISTING WALL

EXISTING RWP TO BE CUT SHORT TO DISCHARGE ONTO NEW ROOF

EXISTING M&E EQUIPMENT SERVICING ADJOINING PREMISES

GLAZED ROOF TO STAIR

AIR BRICK VENTS TO BOILER ROOM

k KITCHEN EXTRACT FAN AND FLUE

PARTY WALL RAISED

PANEL OF PAINTED PLY

GUTTER

PAINTED DOOR

RENDERED BLOCKWORK

EXISTING PARAPET WALL & ROOF OUTLET

NEW ROOF

NEW ROOF

ELEVATION Z Z

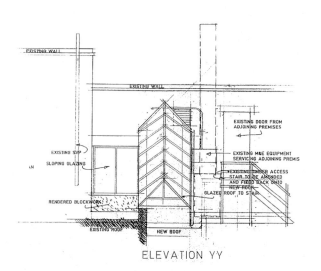

EXISTING WALL

EXISTING WALL

EXISTING DOOR FROM ADJOINING PREMISES

EXISTING M&E EQUIPMENT SERVICING ADJOINING PREMIS

EXISTING SVP

SLOPING GLAZING

EXISTING TIMBER ACCESS STAIR TO BE AMENDED AND FIXED BACK ONTO NEW ROOF

GLAZED ROOF TO STAIR

RENDERED BLOCKWORK

EXISTING ROOF

NEW ROOF

ELEVATION YY

The restaurant is divided into three distinct rooms, taking advantage of the existing structure of the building.

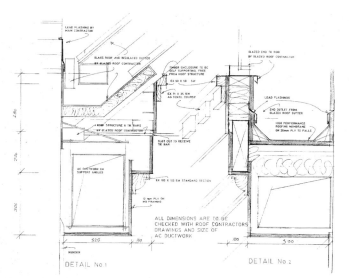

Detail of the meeting of the roof and the façade.

One of the main spaces created by gutting and fitting out the building is the covered terrace at the rear of the building. In summer, half the skylight is moved sideways by an electric device until it is placed on top of the other half. In the diagram below, the layout and cross sections of the terrace. On the opposite page, a general view.

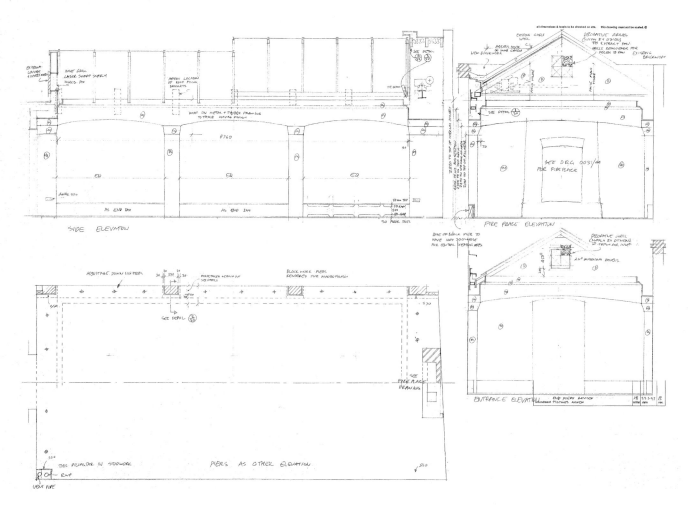

Location: *89 Mercer Street, New York, Estados Unidos.*
Year of opening: *1995.*
Client: *NY 93 Corp.*
Architects: *Gilles Depardon, Kathryn Ogawa.*
Collaborator: *Dawn Finley.*
Structure: *Hage Engineering.*
Mechanics: *Sigma Engineering.*
Lighting: *Lighting Dynamics.*
Interior design and sculpture: *Janis Leonard.*
Curtain wall: *Perry Chin.*

Set within the historic Cast Iron District of New York's Soho, the restaurant is located in a two story building on a small plot of land, 23 ft. wide and 90 ft. deep, between two six floor buildings which have a very imposing presence on the urban landscape.

The 89 consists of two stories which are simply defined by very few architectural elements: the façade and entrance, the bar, the skylight, the staircase, and the restaurant. The curved geometry and the deliberately sought-after transparency of all the elements emphasize the continuity between the inside and outside, and between the different zones of the bar. This is even noticeable in the smallest details.

When one is in the street, the glass façade invites the pedestrians to look inside. At the same time, but looking in the other direction, the cast iron buildings seem to be a stage set across which the pedestrians pass.

Inside, the skylight not only allows daylight to enter, but also it allows the adjoining terraces of the neighbouring workshops to be contemplated. The softly curved staircase, which imitates the geometry of the bar and of the skylight, leads the clients up into the attic lounge, the most intimate part of the restaurant.

Like a modern grafting onto the historic fabric of Soho, the architecture of the 89 tries to reflect the transition from the old to the new, from inside to outside, between the light and the shadows of the views.

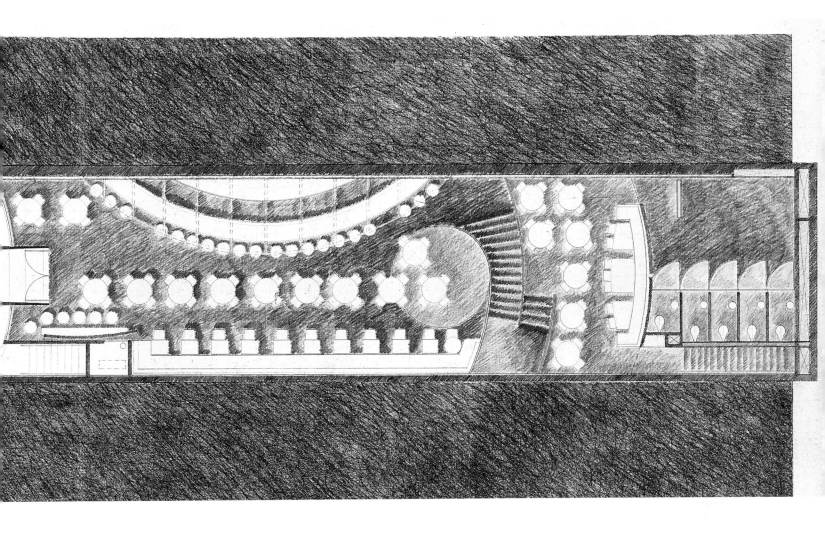

Although the height of the restaurant gives the impression that the relationship with the adjoining buildings was not studied, this drawing shows that in fact they did take this into consideration. Actually, in spite of the undeniable differences, the decision to make the metal structure stand out is in part a tribute to the surroundings.

General layout. The architects have tried to ensure that there are few visual barriers. Their objective was to create a well-lit open space with a direct view of the street.

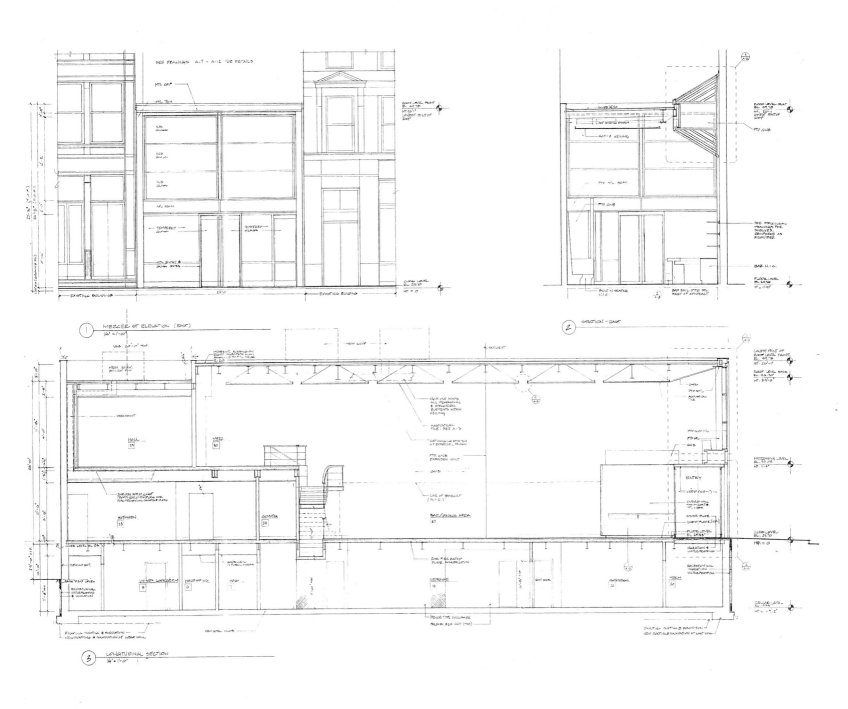

The bar imitates the curved form of the skylight.

Elevation of the entrance, cross and longitudinal sections.

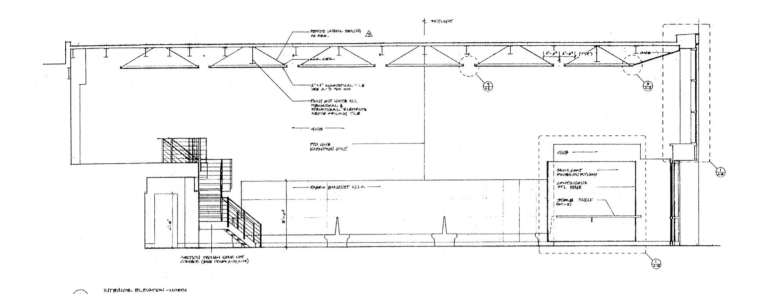

① INTERIOR ELEVATION – NORTH
1/4" = 1'-0"

On this page and the next, the two interior elevations.

The two interior walls are practically bare. One result is to convert the wall below the skylight into a screen that reflects the light. In addition, the visitor can immediately take in the space from the moment that they enter.

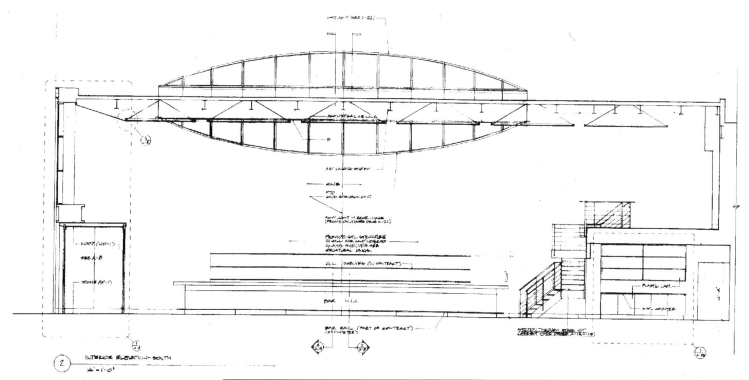

The rest rooms of the 89 are one of the most curious areas in the restaurant. When they are empty the glass door is transparent. However, when someone goes in they become opaque so that you can not see in from outside.

A view of the structure of the façade. The restaurant has a double street door so that heat does not escape in winter. This has created a small, gallery like space on both sides of the entrance.

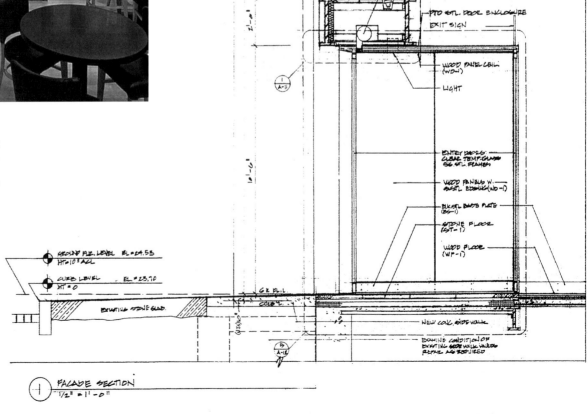

After the skylight the most arresting visual feature of the restaurant is the stairway leading to the upper floor, whose curved shape is not frequent in the todays architecture, but is found in the neighbouring buildings built at the begining of the century. Ogawa and Depardon thus establish another point of connection with the surroundings.

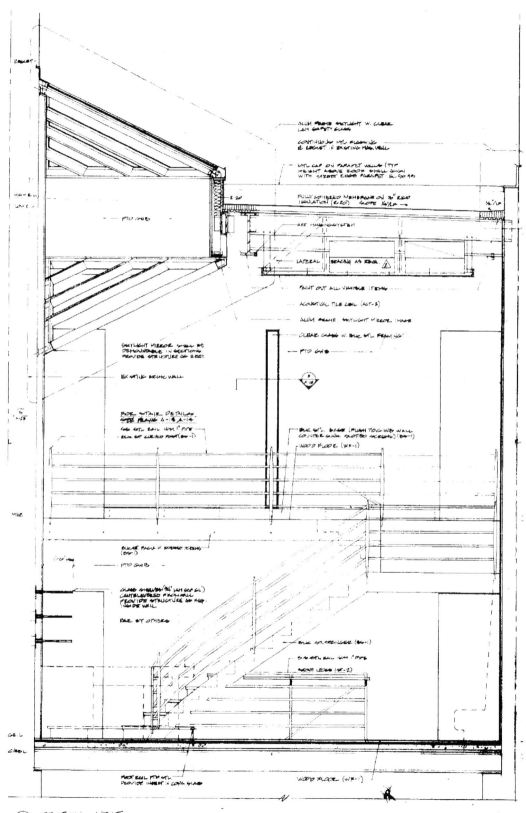

SECTION - WEST
1/2" = 1'-0"

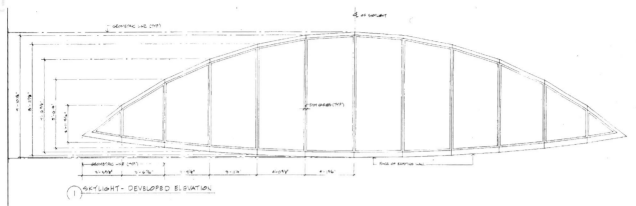

① SKYLIGHT - DEVELOPED ELEVATION

③ SKYLIGHT - PLAN

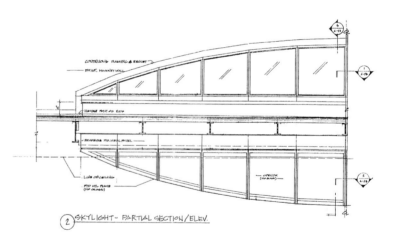

② SKYLIGHT - PARTIAL SECTION/ELEV.

As can be observed in these plans, and in the photo on the left, the skylight is made up of two sheets of glass and a chamber in the middle. This has solved the problem of condensation, which is so common in these type of elements.

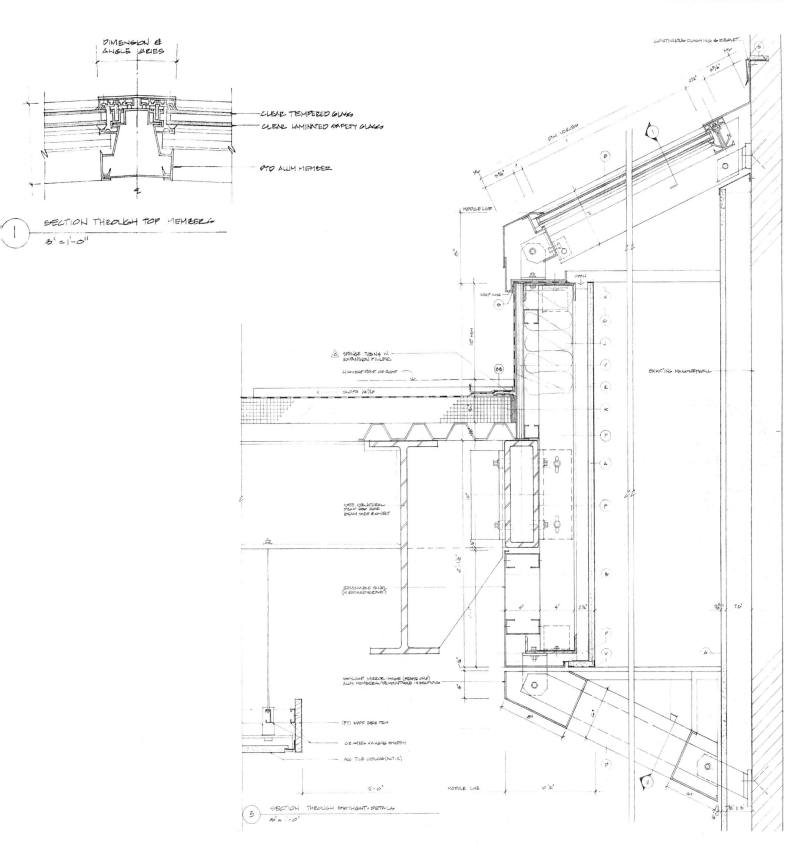

DIMENSION &
ANGLE VARIES

CLEAR TEMPERED GLASS
CLEAR LAMINATED SAFETY GLASS

STD ALUM MEMBER

SECTION THROUGH TOP MEMBERS

① 3" = 1'-0"

CONTINUOUS FLASHING & REGLET

MODULE LINE

SPONGE TUBING W.
EXPANSION FILLER

HIGHEST POINT OF ROOF

SLOPE 1/4"/LF

SEE STRUCTURAL
PLAN FOR
BEAM SIZE & CONFIG

EXISTING MASONRY WALL

REMOVABLE PANEL
(W. EXPOSED SCREWS)

SKYLIGHT MIRROR IMAGE (FRAME ONLY)
ALUM MEMBERS / OR MOUNTING IN SECTION

(PT) WOOD BASE TRIM

GR. STEEL HANGING SYSTEM

ACC TILE CEILING (ACT-2)

2'-0"   MODULE LINE   10 1/2"

③ **SECTION THROUGH SKYLIGHT - DETAILS**

10 1/2" = 1'-0"

Paul Haigh

Location: *Manhattan, New York, United States.*
Year of opening: *1993.*
Client: *Caroline Hirsch.*
Cost: U.S.$*1,5 million.*
Design: *Paul Haigh, Barbara H. Haigh.*
Collaborators: *Nicholas Macri, Miriana Donaya, Justin Bologna,*
Karla Kuperc; CMA Enterprises (constructor).

Located in Times Square, the theatre district of Manhattan, this 18,000 sq.ft. premises includes a small theatre for 300 people and a restaurant for 80. It was specially designed for comedies to be represented, always trying to ensure that the audience was close to the actors, as if it were a great living room. On nights when there is a small attendance the theatre can be sub-divided so that the sensation of intimacy is not lost.

The entrance is from Broadway, by going down some stairs that lead to the basement where the room is located. The route is like a guided tour, for as the visitor moves along they are introduced to the neomedieval world of harlequins, pantomine and jokers. This iconography of colors and distincly varied decoration runs all over the club in different forms and scales. Paul Haigh has used velvet tapestries, stained and colored woods, terrazo floors and fitted carpets to achieve this effect.

The basement is divided into two zones by a curved wall. On one side there is the theatre with three blocks of curved, staggered seats. On the other side the restaurant is found, which also serves as a foyer.

This division, which is obligatory during the shows, does not prevent there being a fluid relation between both zones. The bar-restaurant is made up of a series of small separate areas that are joined by wide corridors in which performances occasionally take place. Moreover, it is not difficult to sit down next to the actors who have just been on the stage, as if you were dining in the wings of the theatre.

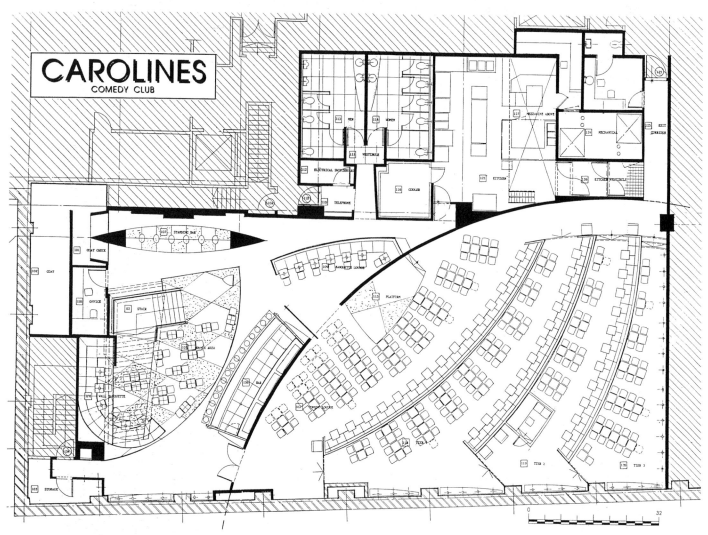

CAROLINES
COMEDY CLUB

A curved wall divides the club into two zones: the restaurant and the theatre. This curved line decides the shape of the rest of the elements in the club: the bar, the chairs, etc.

Paul Haigh used the geometry of the suits of the harlequins to decorate the walls, the benches and the tables.

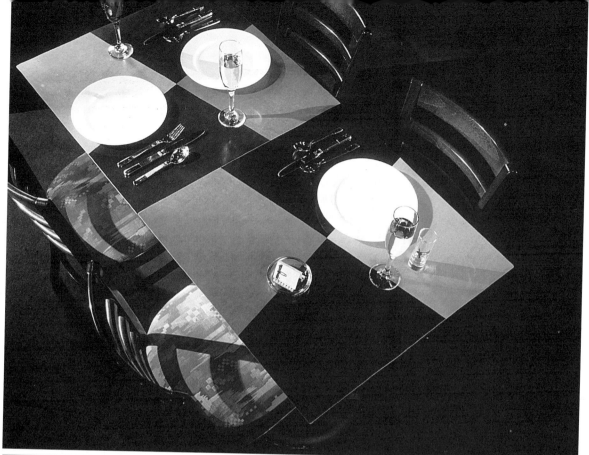

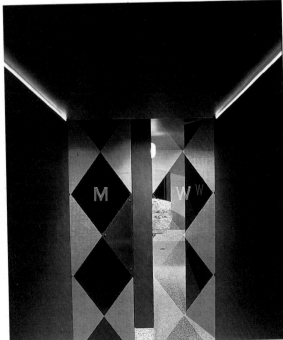

Caroline's Club is located in a basement. Therefore, it has no natural light and the way the artificial light is treated is one of the most important ingredients of Paul Haigh's project. Not only was the placing and the type of lamps studied, but also reflecting surfaces were fitted which would increase the luminosity and color of the premises.

The fly shaped stools are some of the most characteristic furniture of the club.

On entering, patrons are confronted with the stairs which act as an extension of the doors and a prologue to the restaurant, containing as it does the main themes of the design: the use of rhombords, the cromatic treatment, etc.

As the stair plan shows, the stairs do not descend paralell to the stairwell, allowing the visitor to glimpse the club as they descend.

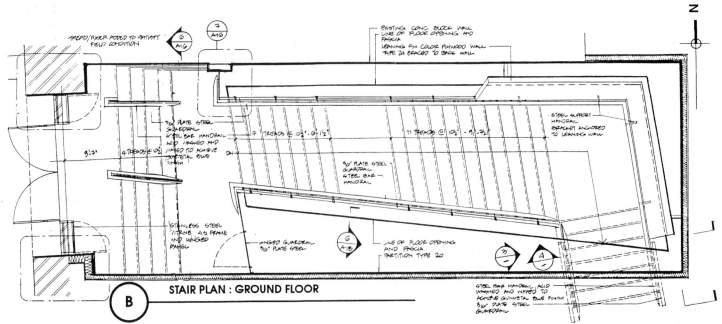

STAIR PLAN : GROUND FLOOR

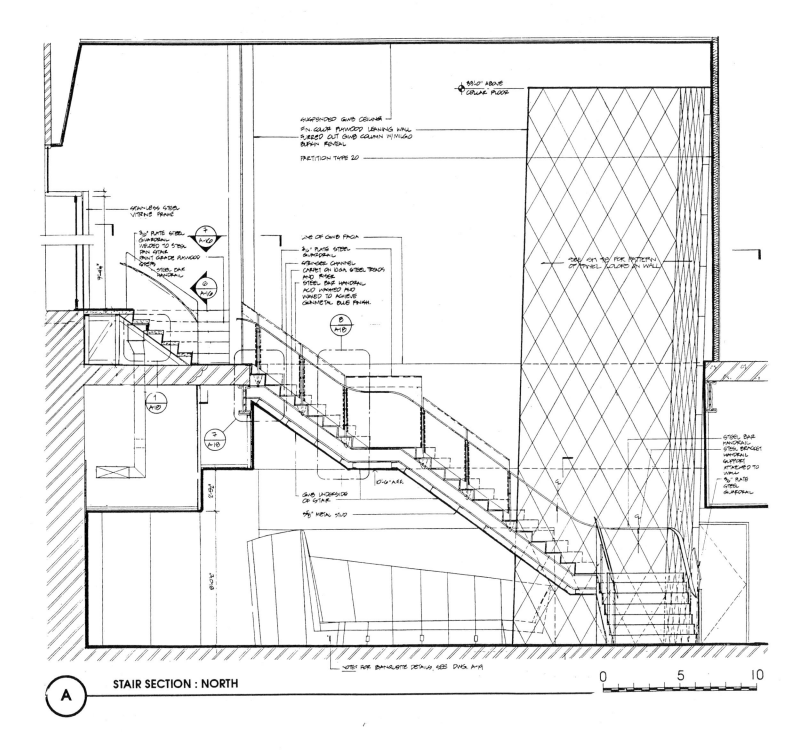

Oxo Tower

Lifschutz Davidson

Location: *London, United Kingdom.*
Year of opening: *1997.*
Client: *Harvey Nichols.*
Design: *Lifschutz Davidson.*
Constructor: *John Sisk & Sons.*
Structural engineers: *Buro Happold/WSP.*
Construction services: *Mecserve/How Engineering.*
Lighting: *Equation Lighting Design.*
Quality control: *EC Harris and Partners.*

Since 1930 the Oxo Tower has been a landmark on the Thames waterfront. This art deco building, a former post office and meat warehouse, enjoys one of the best views of the river.

In recent years the building has been refurbished to accommodate a number of very different activities. The first three floors are given over to commerce, and another five are occupied by seventy eight apartments. Finally, the top floor houses the two restaurants (eatery and brasserie) and the Harvey Nichols bar.

Aware of the exceptional view offered by the restaurant, the Lifschutz Davidson architects built a light roof supported by lattice beams that in turn rest on two pillars standing in the middle of the building. The kitchens, the services, and the storerooms are also in the central area. In this way the whole façade is freed from any vertical or horizontal element that might spoil the view. The roof slopes slightly north-south, so the façade over the Thames is considerably higher than the one overlooking the Bargehouse building.

The glass skin has practically no uprights nor frames. Guys attached to the roof support the intermediate anchors of the window panes. Thus, the first three metres of the façade are completely transparent.

The underside of the roof consists of slats that are opened and closed by a motor. This method makes it possible not only to control the acoustics (which is essential in establishments of this size), but also to adjust the reflection of sunlight to regulate the intensity and color of the light.

General section of the building.

1. Restaurant.
2. Terrace.
3. Apartments.
4. Central corridor.
5. Walkway.
6. Workshops.
7. Shopping mall.
8. Bargehouse building.

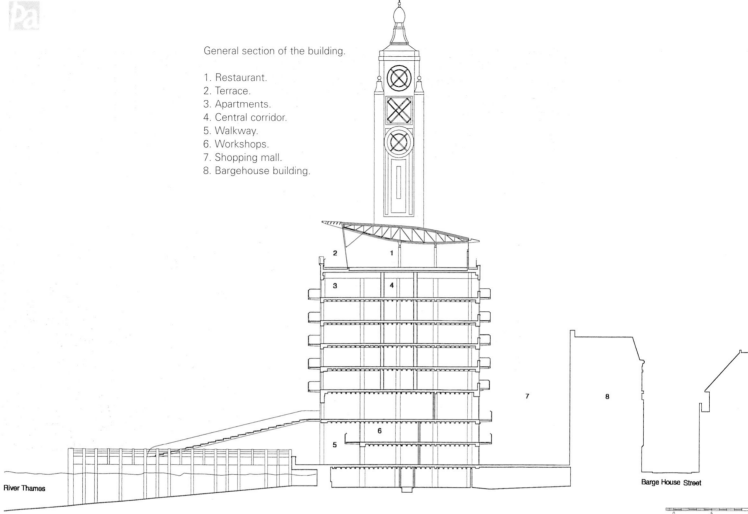

River Thames

Barge House Street

From the terrace, situated on the ninth floor, you can enjoy some splendid views over the River Thames and the dome of Saint Paul's Cathedral.

In fact the restaurant is comprised of two restaurants (one of them is a brasserie) under the same name, but each one has its own kitchen, toilets and bar.

General layout.

1. Brasserie.
2. Bar.
3. Restaurant.
4. Kitchen.
5. Elevator.
6. Goods elevator.
7. Viewing point.
8. Terrace.
9. Recepction.
10. Distribution area.
11. Plant.

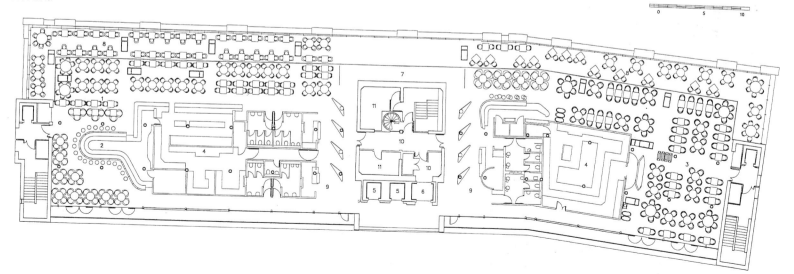

TERRACE SEATING AREA BRASSERIE BAR terrace

RESIDENTIAL CORRIDOR RESIDENTIAL

Cross section.
The double roof allows the air conditioning ducts to be installed. By the same measure, a system of slats that are opened and closed by a motor enable the late afternoon sunlight to be controlled.

The closing of the windows has been designed in such a way that the uprights hardly spoil the clear view.

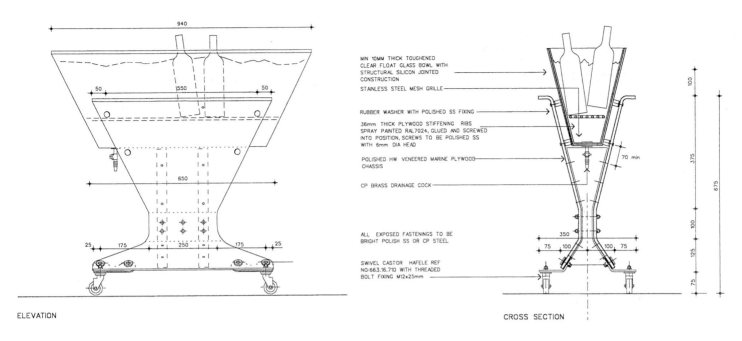

940

50   1550   50

650

25   175   250   175   25

ELEVATION

MIN 10MM THICK TOUGHENED
CLEAR FLOAT GLASS BOWL WITH
STRUCTURAL SILICON JOINTED
CONSTRUCTION

STAINLESS STEEL MESH GRILLE

RUBBER WASHER WITH POLISHED SS FIXING

36mm THICK PLYWOOD STIFFENING RIBS
SPRAY PAINTED RAL7024, GLUED AND SCREWED
INTO POSITION, SCREWS TO BE POLISHED SS
WITH 6mm DIA HEAD

POLISHED HW VENEERED MARINE PLYWOOD
CHASSIS

CP BRASS DRAINAGE COCK

ALL EXPOSED FASTENINGS TO BE
BRIGHT POLISH SS OR CP STEEL

SWIVEL CASTOR HAFELE REF
NO:663.16.710 WITH THREADED
BOLT FIXING M12x25mm

100

375

675

100

125

70 min

350

75   100   100   75

75

CROSS SECTION

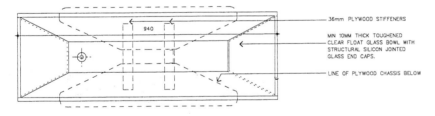

940

36mm PLYWOOD STIFFENERS

MIN 10MM THICK TOUGHENED
CLEAR FLOAT GLASS BOWL WITH
STRUCTURAL SILICON JOINTED
GLASS END CAPS.

LINE OF PLYWOOD CHASSIS BELOW

PLAN - TOP LEVEL

This is a drawing of the construction of
the ice bucket, and a finished photo. It
was designed by the team of architects themselves.

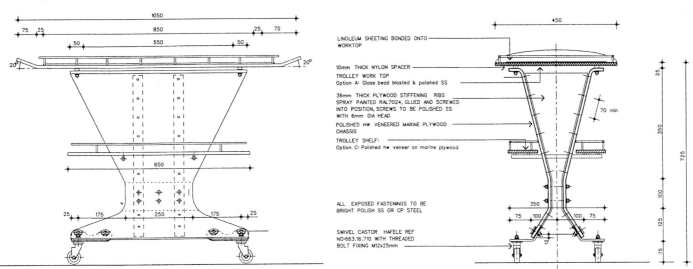

ELEVATION

CROSS SECTION

LINOLEUM SHEETING BONDED ONTO WORKTOP

10mm THICK NYLON SPACER

TROLLEY WORK TOP
Option A: Glass bead blasted & polished SS

36mm THICK PLYWOOD STIFFENING RIBS SPRAY PAINTED RAL7024, GLUED AND SCREWED INTO POSITION, SCREWS TO BE POLISHED SS WITH 6mm DIA HEAD

POLISHED HW VENEERED MARINE PLYWOOD CHASSIS

TROLLEY SHELF:
Option C: Polished hw veneer on marine plywood

ALL EXPOSED FASTENINGS TO BE BRIGHT POLISH SS OR CP STEEL

SWIVEL CASTOR HAFELE REF NO:663.16.710 WITH THREADED BOLT FIXING M12x25mm

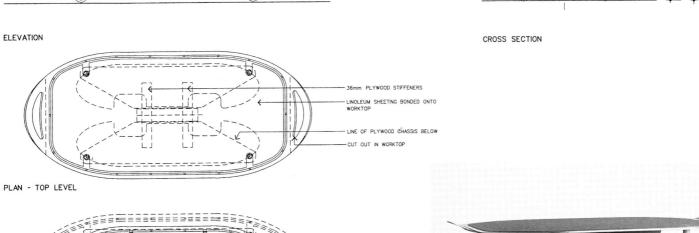

PLAN - TOP LEVEL

36mm PLYWOOD STIFFENERS

LINOLEUM SHEETING BONDED ONTO WORKTOP

LINE OF PLYWOOD CHASSIS BELOW

CUT OUT IN WORKTOP

PLAN - LOWER LEVEL

LINE OF WORKTOP ABOVE

LINE OF CHASSIS BELOW

6mm DIAMETER POLISHED SS TUBULAR RAIL TO SHELF

A close up of one of the service trays.

Francesc Rifé

Location: *Terrassa, Barcelona, Spain.*
Design: *Francesc Rifé.*
Year of opening: *1997.*

These premises were dedicated to the sale of products related to coffee. As it is in a downtown pedestrian street, with many people passing by, the idea of a quick access, open door establishment came to mind. The door leading to the neighbours' staircase had to be integrated, and this aided a great deal in designing the façade.

The premises consist of two spaces joined together by a funnel like zone caused by the unchangeable positioning of the staircase leading up to the private apartments. This handicap was overcome by creating a semi-circular false ceiling that joined the two zones. The part that gives out onto the street has a bar where the clients can stand, and at the rear they can take a coffee sitting down. The rest rooms and storerooms are also here. The air conditioning ducts and the embedded lighting were housed in the ceiling.

The designers thought of the idea of a display case to unify the two zones, with the aim of creating a cultural atmosphere by putting on rotating exhibitions, and thus complementing the atmosphere of the café. This show case has been designed using tubular uprights finished in varnished stainless steel, which create square units with reinforced one-piece glass doors. The lower part is clamped into the floor which is covered by a coffee colored carpet.

The bar at the front starts in the street, inviting the passer-by to enter the café, and follows the line of the false ceiling. The front of the bar has been covered with vertical slats of dyed beechwood, and the top of the counter is of white, stain-resistant marble.

The façade, like the interior, has been covered with limestone, blending in with the aluminium sign. Additionally, by the doormat a plant has been placed to welcome in the clients, and to separate off the two entrances from each other.

A view of the coffee drinking area. The aim was to avoid going too far with the lighting, so that the atmosphere was relaxing.

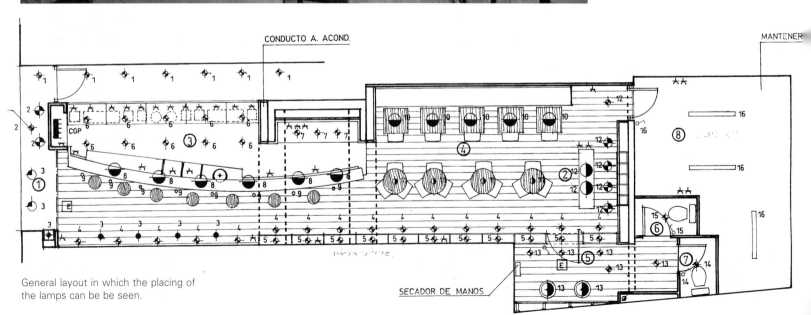

CONDUCTO A. ACOND.

MANTENER

SECADOR DE MANOS

General layout in which the placing of the lamps can be be seen.

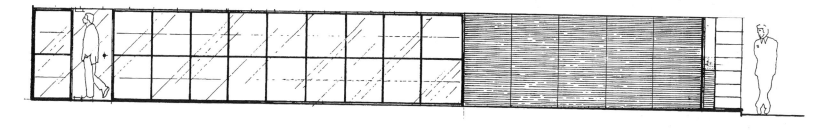

The premises are narrow and deep. This is why the treatment given to the side walls was one of the most important issues in the project.

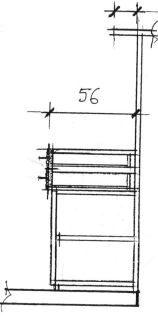

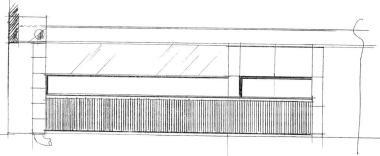

The bar reaches to the street. The plan is that, when the climate so permits, the doors will remain open thus taking the café into the street.

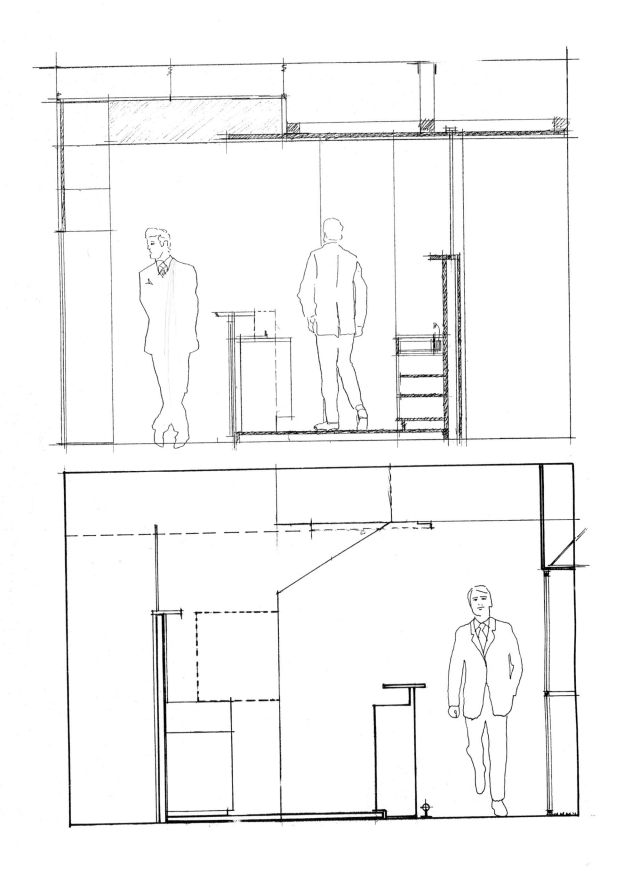

The bar being curved means that the client does not have the sensation of going along a passage. At the same time, great care was taken in the way the section was finished off, the height of the objects and the way they were seen from the customers' view point.

Francesc Rifé took advantage of a wide stretch of the establishment to fit in the rest rooms. The side wall show case continues and therefore the rest rooms can be seen through the glass. On the back wall of the toilet, a mirror throws back a reflection which creates a complex superimposition of planes.

Jeffrey Beers

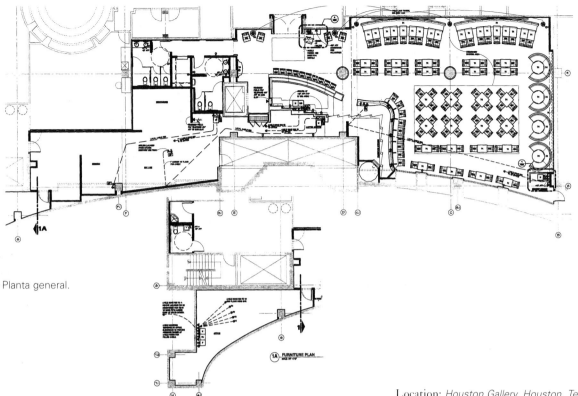

Planta general.

Location: *Houston Gallery, Houston, Texas, United States.*
Year of opening: *1997.*
Client: *Bruce y Susan Molzan.*
Design: *Jeffrey Beers Architecture and design.*

Located on the second floor of the Houston Gallery, in the department store of Saks Fifth Avenue, managed by Ruggles, this 5,000 sq. ft. restaurant was planned not only to serve meals to the staff and shopping customers, but also as a place which would be visited for its own sake, to have dinner and spend a relaxed evening. Therefore, the elevator takes the clients directly from the street to the restaurant.

Furthermore, the ambience and decor are far more luxurious than is habitual in this type of restaurant.

The kitchen is laid out with an open, marble and stainless steel counter. The bar merges into the counter of the kitchen and winds around one of the corners of the the establishment.

The atmosphere of all the restaurant is heavily influenced by the carefully chosen floor and ceiling. On the ground, the team of Jeffrey Beers designed a complex pattern of white, black and grey tones.

The lighting is set in rectangular blocks in the plaster ceiling. A line of fluorescent lights hidden in the false ceiling bathes the room in a soft light. Some resin lamps hung from a quasi-chandelier by a gold-leaf tube accentuate the warm light of the restaurant, making them the most striking elements of the decor of the establishment.

The curtains at the end of the room, the white table cloths, the leather covered chairs and benches put the final touches to the luxury and exquisiteness of this art decor setting.

The care taken even with the smallest details is reflected in the least visible elements. The entrance door, for example, when opened, fits completely into the side wall. A small hollow has been made to allow for the handle.

The bar (photo on the opposite page) has a small eating ledge. The construction plan reveals the choice of warm materials.

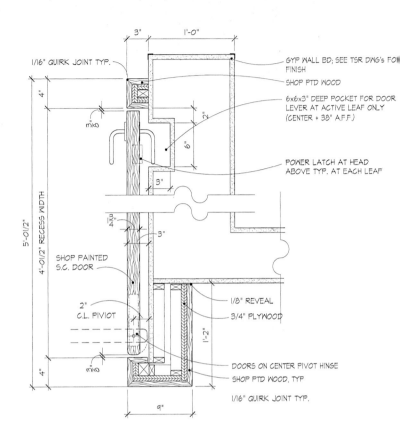

GYP WALL BD; SEE TSR DWG's FOR FINISH

SHOP PTD WOOD

6x6x3" DEEP POCKET FOR DOOR LEVER AT ACTIVE LEAF ONLY (CENTER + 38" A.F.F.)

POWER LATCH AT HEAD ABOVE TYP. AT EACH LEAF

1/16" QUIRK JOINT TYP.

4"

3"

1'-0"

2"

6"

3"

5'-01/2" RECESS WIDTH

4'-01/2" RECESS WIDTH

3/4"

3"

SHOP PAINTED S.C. DOOR

1/8" REVEAL

3/4" PLYWOOD

2" C.L. PIVIOT

1'-2"

4"

9"

DOORS ON CENTER PIVOT HINGE

SHOP PTD WOOD, TYP

1/16" QUIRK JOINT TYP.

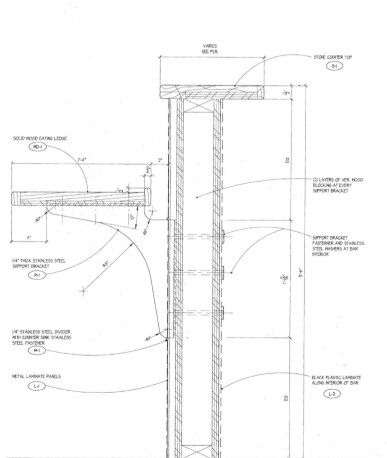

VARIES SEE PLN.

STONE COUNTER TOP
S-1

SOLID WOOD EATING LEDGE
W-1

1'-4"

2"

(2) LAYERS OF VER. WOOD BLOCKING AT EVERY SUPPORT BRACKET

4"

SUPPORT BRACKET FASTENER AND STAINLESS STEEL WASHERS AT BAR INTERIOR

1/4" THICK STAINLESS STEEL SUPPORT BRACKET
M-1

3'-4"

1/4" STAINLESS STEEL DIVIDER WITH COUNTER SUNK STAINLESS STEEL FASTENER
M-1

METAL LAMINATE PANELS
L-1

BLACK PLASTIC LAMINATE ALONG INTERIOR OF BAR
L-2

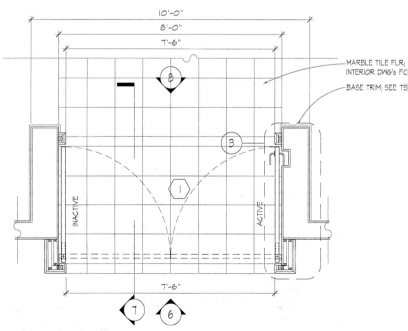

10'-0"

8'-0"

7'-6"

MARBLE TILE FLR; INTERIOR DWG's FOR

BASE TRIM; SEE TS

8

3

INACTIVE

ACTIVE

1

7'-6"

7

6

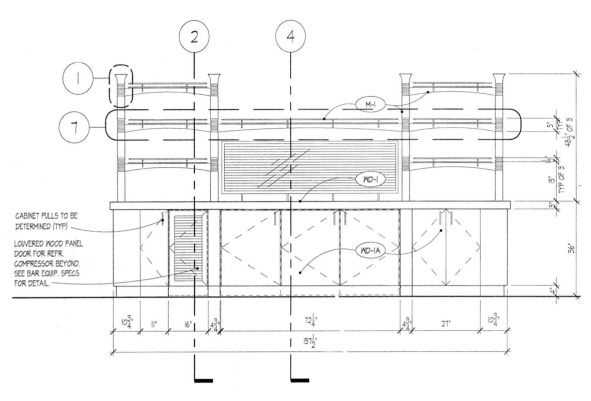

CABINET PULLS TO BE
DETERMINED (TYP)

LOUVERED WOOD PANEL
DOOR FOR REFR.
COMPRESSOR BEYOND.
SEE BAR EQUIP. SPECS
FOR DETAIL.

M-1

WD-1

WD-1A

An elevation of the Gentleman's bar,
situated on the upper floor, and a close
up of the metal upright of the glass
showcase behind the bar counter.

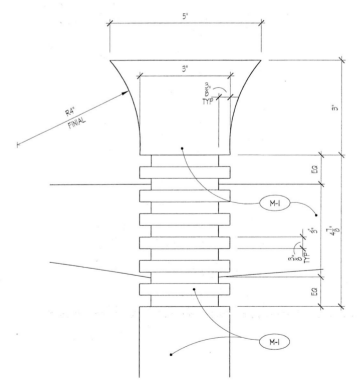

On the next page, construction plans
of the bar. As can be seen, the vertical
face is formed by an onyx panel with
metal supports and is lit from behind.

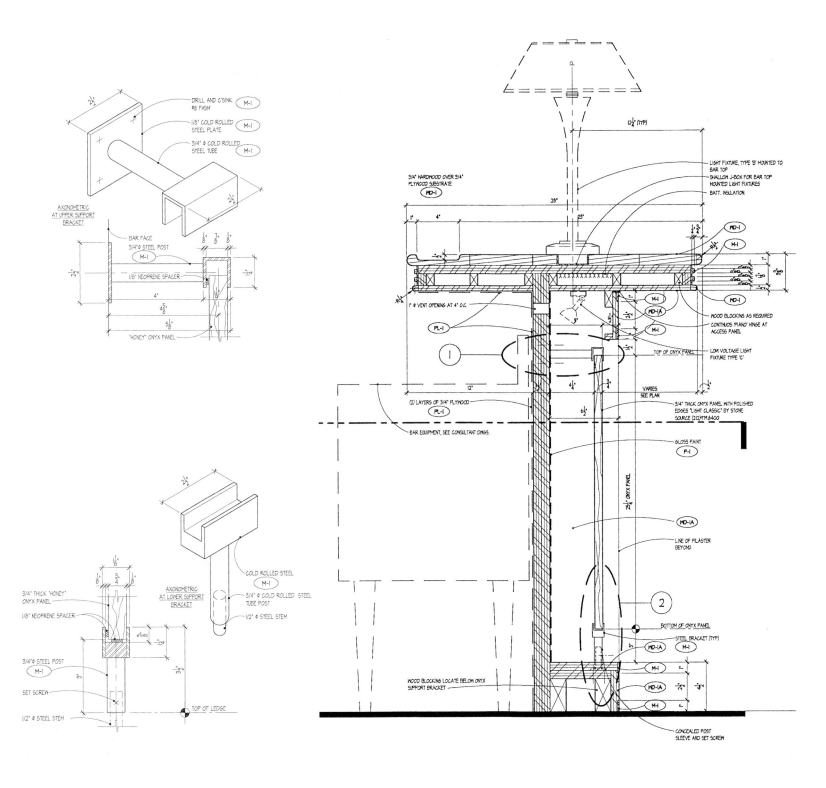

AXONOMETRIC
AT UPPER SUPPORT
BRACKET

DRILL AND C'SINK
#8 FHSM — M-1

1/8" COLD ROLLED
STEEL PLATE — M-1

3/4" Ø COLD ROLLED
STEEL TUBE — M-1

BAR FACE
3/4"Ø STEEL POST — M-1

1/8" NEOPRENE SPACER

"HONEY" ONYX PANEL

AXONOMETRIC
AT LOWER SUPPORT
BRACKET

COLD ROLLED STEEL — M-1

3/4" Ø COLD ROLLED STEEL
TUBE POST

1/2" Ø STEEL STEM

3/4" THICK "HONEY"
ONYX PANEL

1/8" NEOPRENE SPACER

3/4"Ø STEEL POST — M-1

SET SCREW

1/2" Ø STEEL STEM

TOP OF LEDGE

3/4" HARDWOOD OVER 3/4"
PLYWOOD SUBSTRATE — MD-1

LIGHT FIXTURE, TYPE 'B' MOUNTED TO
BAR TOP

SHALLOW J-BOX FOR BAR TOP
MOUNTED LIGHT FIXTURES

BATT. INSULATION

1" Ø VENT OPENING AT 4" O.C.

WOOD BLOCKING AS REQUIRED

CONTINUOUS PIANO HINGE AT
ACCESS PANEL

TOP OF ONYX PANEL

LOW VOLTAGE LIGHT
FIXTURE TYPE 'C'

(2) LAYERS OF 3/4" PLYWOOD — PL-1

BAR EQUIPMENT, SEE CONSULTANT DWGS.

3/4" THICK ONYX PANEL WITH POLISHED
EDGES 'LIGHT CLASSIC' BY STONE
SOURCE (212) XXX-XXXX

GLOSS PAINT — P-1

LINE OF PILASTER
BEYOND

BOTTOM OF ONYX PANEL

STEEL BRACKET (TYP)

WOOD BLOCKING LOCATE BELOW ONYX
SUPPORT BRACKET

CONCEALED POST
SLEEVE AND SET SCREW

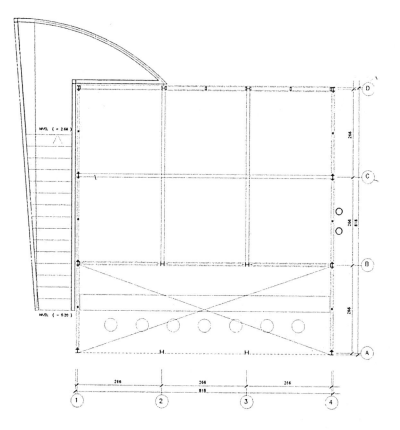

Location: *Puerto de Iquique, Chile.*
Design: *Mathias Klotz & Felipe Assadi*
Year of opening: *1998.*

The Zoficentro units are six mobile restaurants designed for an industrial park in the port of Iquique, 1,200 m north of Santiago.

The commission consisted of developing a mobile structure that could be dismantled, transferred and reinstalled in different points of the park.

The units had to offer a kitchen space, bath rooms, telephone boxes and a shady area with tables.

The solution that the project came up with was a 25x25x25 ft. metal cube structure with plywood panels.

On the ground floor the functions have been separated. The toilets and telephone boxes are at the back, the kitchen in the centre and the restaurant at the front. Up above is the eating terrace.

The cube has two opaque faces and two semi light permeable which are covered by aluminum latticework to allow the wind through but to filter the sun. On the outside a metal staircase has been fitted hanging from two cables.

The cube is closed at night by bringing down two mobile panels that are used as doors at night and as shade during the day.

The idea of a terrace above the kitchen, so forming a balcony over the bar sector, comes from traditional Iquique architecture which worked with wooden sun screens for the terraces.

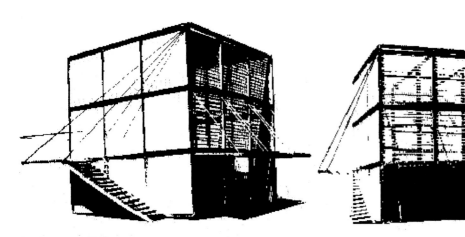

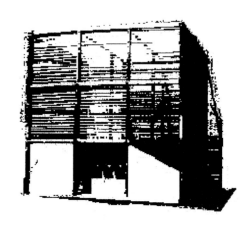

The unit is a perfect 25x25x25 ft. cube. It is designed to be a piece of furniture, and does not need to be placed in any specific place.

On the next page, plans of the four elevations of the unit. You can clearly see that the front and back parts are well defined.

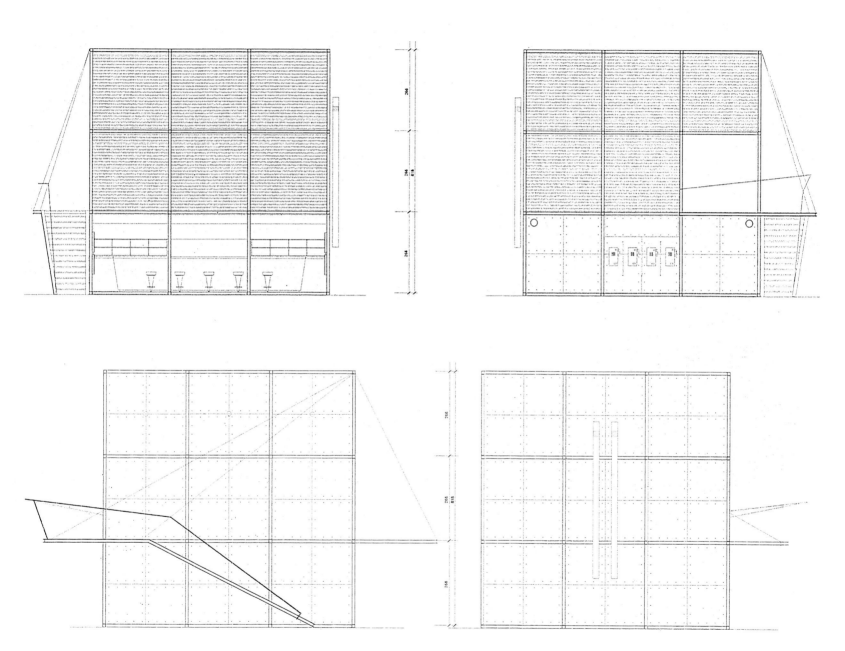

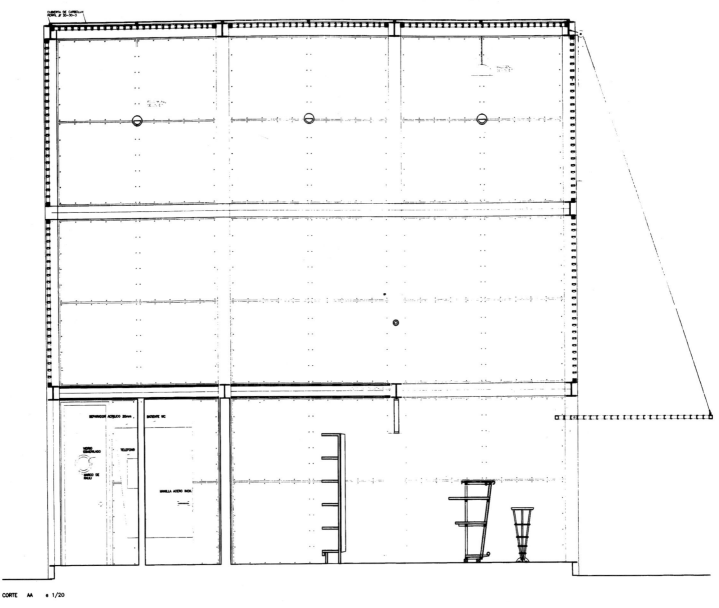

CORTE AA e 1/20

Construction cross section.

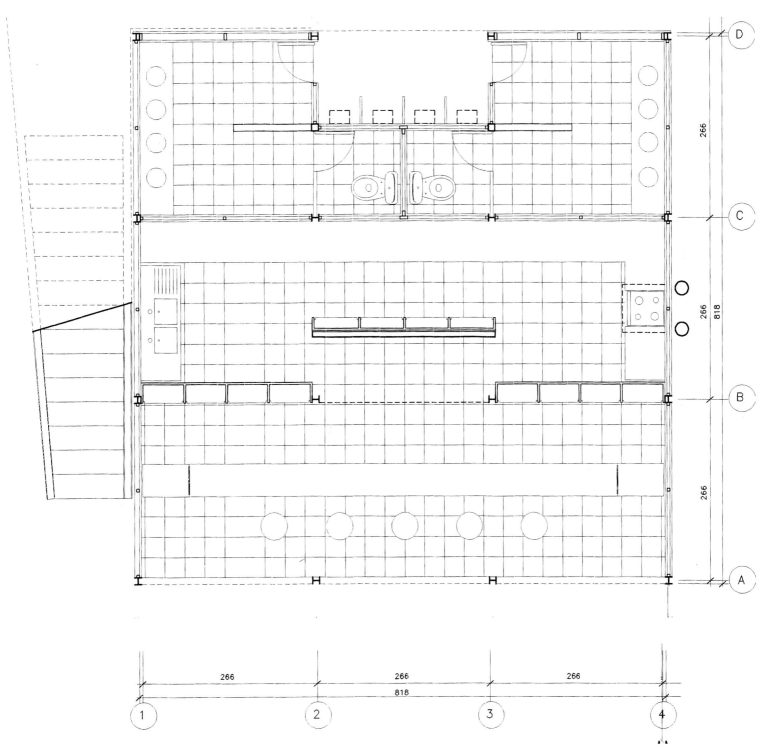

General layout.

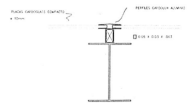

PLACAS CARBOGLASS COMPACTO
e 10mm

PERFILES CARBOLUX ALUMINIO

☐ 0.05 x 0.03 x 003

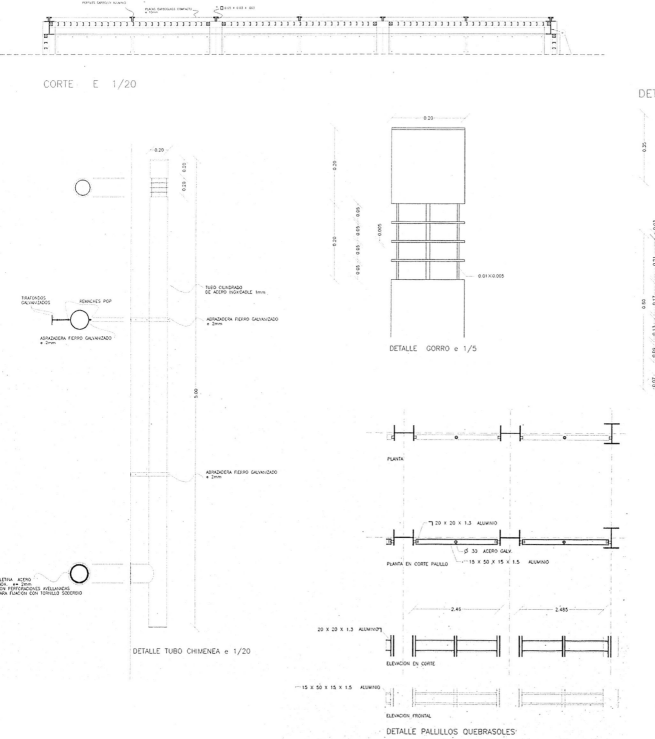

PERFILES CARBOLUX ALUMINIO

PLACAS CARBOGLASS COMPACTO

☐ 0.05 x 0.03 x 003

CORTE   E 1/20

DETALLE   E 1/5

PLANTA PISO BARRA e 1/10

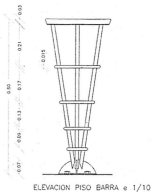

ELEVACION PISO BARRA e 1/10

0.20

TUBO CILINDRADO
DE ACERO INOXIDABLE 1mm

ABRAZADERA FIERRO GALVANIZADO
e 2mm

TIRAFONDOS
GALVANIZADOS

REMACHES POP

ABRAZADERA FIERRO GALVANIZADO
e 2mm

5.00

ABRAZADERA FIERRO GALVANIZADO
e 2mm

PLETINA ACERO
INOX. e= 2mm
CON PERFORACIONES AVELLANADAS
PARA FIJACION CON TORNILLO SOBERBIO

DETALLE TUBO CHIMENEA e 1/20

0.20

0.005

0.01X0.005

DETALLE GORRO e 1/5

PLANTA

20 X 20 X 1.3   ALUMINIO

Ø 30 ACERO GALV.

15 X 50 X 15 X 1.5   ALUMINIO

PLANTA EN CORTE PALILLO

2.46

2.485

20 X 20 X 1.3 ALUMINIO

ELEVACION EN CORTE

15 X 50 X 15 X 1.5   ALUMINIO

ELEVACION FRONTAL

DETALLE PALLILLOS QUEBRASOLES

The structure of steel and wood permits the unit to be set up systematically and ensures a high quality of construction. This seemed the best system for a building that was going to be installed in various locations, some of them far away from Santiago de Chile, where Mathias Klotz's office is. In these two pages the construction plans of the building are shown.

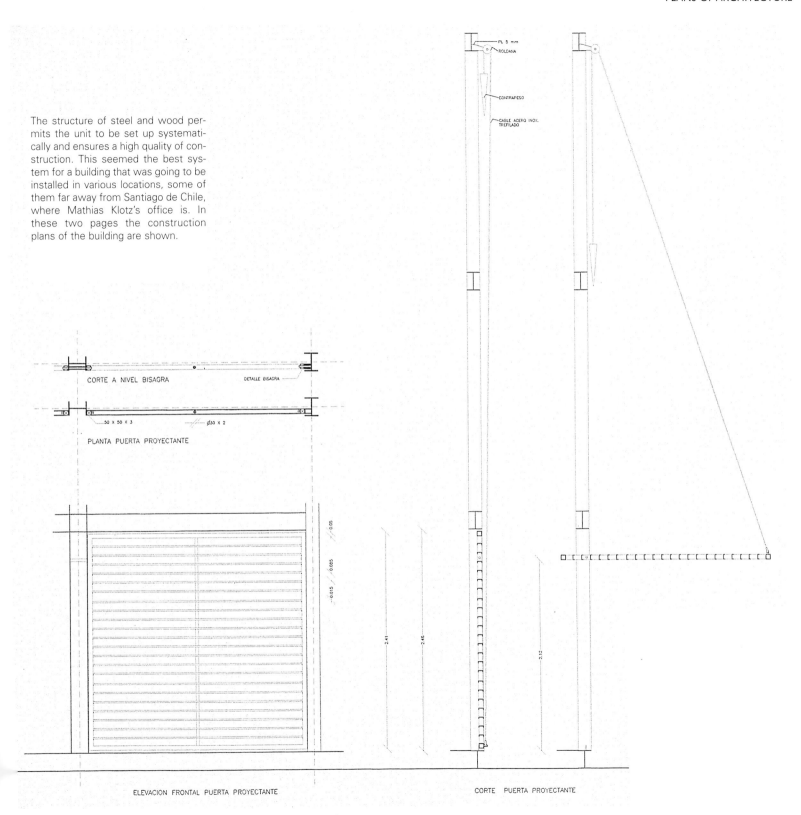

CORTE A NIVEL BISAGRA

DETALLE BISAGRA

PLANTA PUERTA PROYECTANTE

50 X 50 X 3

Ø50 X 2

ELEVACION FRONTAL PUERTA PROYECTANTE

CORTE PUERTA PROYECTANTE

PL 3 mm
ROLDANA
CONTRAPESO
CABLE ACERO INOX. TREFILADO

Cantaloup

Arthur de Mattos

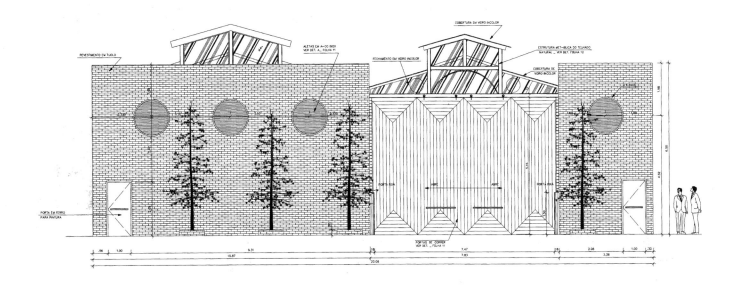

Location: *Rua Manuel Guedes, 474 Sao Paulo, Brazil.*
Year of opening: *1996-1997.*
Design: *Arthur de Mattos Casas.*
Collaborators: *Francisca da Silva, Silvia Carmezzini.*

The space today occupied by the Cantaloup restaurant was in the past a bakery. Some years ago the building suffered a severe fire, which has meant that the structure, designed specifically for the restaurant, is almost completely new.

The restaurant is divided into two bays, clearly differentiated both in the floor plan and the façade. One is occupied by the large dining room and covered by a metal structure with a skylight. The side walls are covered by large scale paintings, the themes of which are gastronomic -food, table layouts, etc. The bar and a small wine cellar occupy the two ends of the room.

The second bay houses the kitchen and a second dining room which can be transformed into an open air garden or, when necessary, be opened up to the main room, thus doubling the capacity.

The roof is formed by a structure of glass and steel which folds back at the touch of a switch, while the façade is composed of two large wooden sliding doors.

In the first year after its inauguration, the Cantaloup became one of the most successful restaurants in Sao Paulo, and its owners decided to enlarge the premises with the addition of an adjoining bar that they named the Cantaloup Living Room, which opened a year later and is housed in an independent building, the atmosphere of which is more intimate.

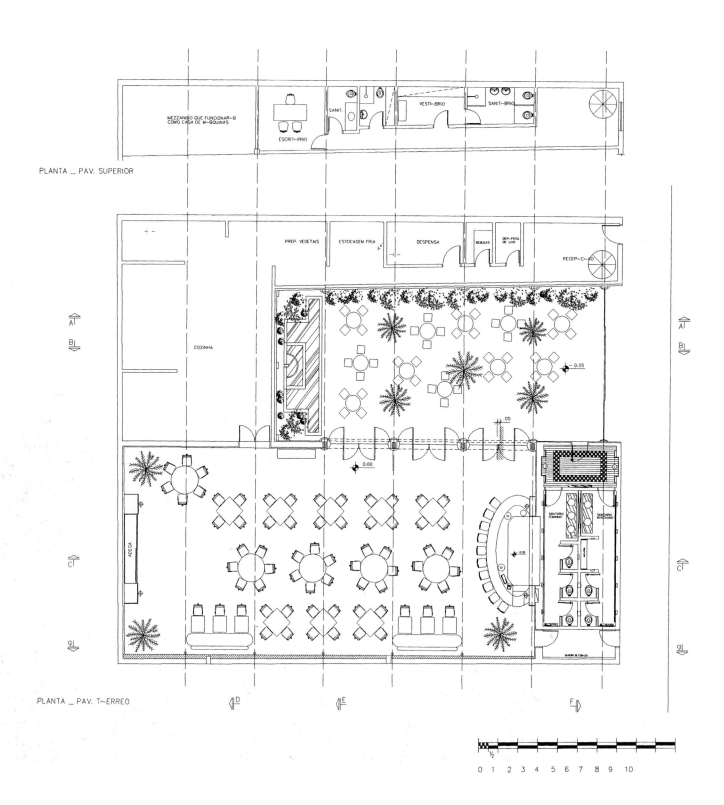

PLANTA _ PAV. SUPERIOR

MEZZANINO QUE FUNCIONAR~B
COMO CASA DE M~BQUINAS

ESCRIT~PRIO

SANIT.

VESTI~BRIO

SANIT~BRIO

PREP. VEGETAIS

ESTOCAGEM FRIA

DESPENSA

BEBIDAS

DEP~PSTO
DE LUXO

RECEP~C~AO

COZINHA

ADEGA

SANITARIO
FEMININO

SANITARIO
MASCULINO

QUADRO DE FOR~CA

- 0.05

.05

0.00

+ 0.30

A

B

C

g

A

B

C

g

PLANTA _ PAV. T~ERREO

D

E

F

½

0 1 2 3 4 5 6 7 8 9 10

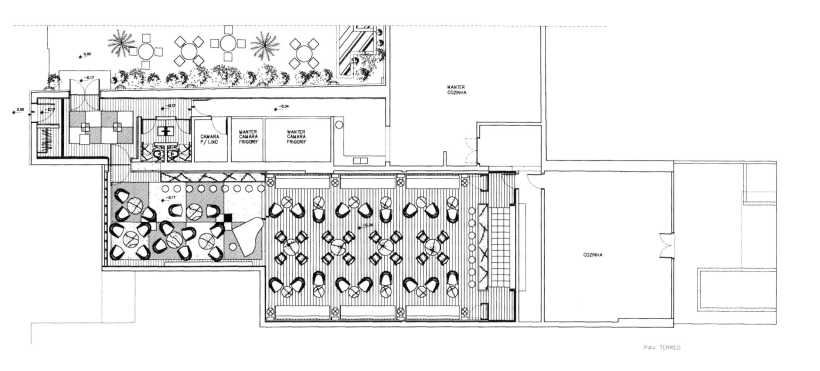

MANTER
COZINHA

CAMARA
P/ LIXO

MANTER
CAMARA
FRIGORIF

MANTER
CAMARA
FRIGORIF

COZINHA

PAV. TERREO

Above, the layout of the extension that was finished in 1997 and was given the name of the Cantaloup Living Room. It is a bar associated with the restaurant that permits the clients to round the night off.

On the previous page, layout of the original project of 1996.

The two photos show views of the two spaces.

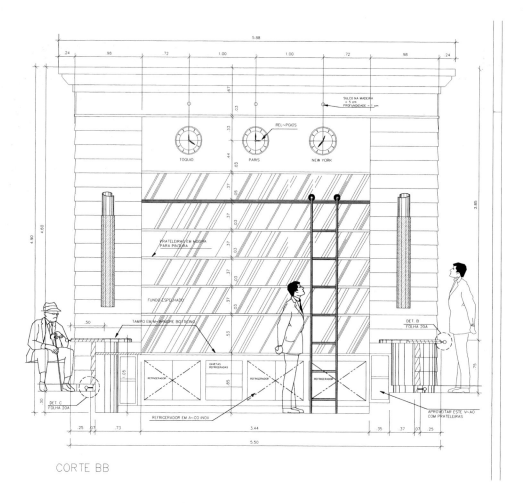

CORTE BB

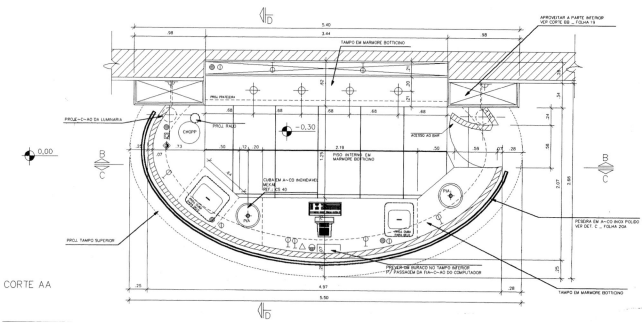

CORTE AA

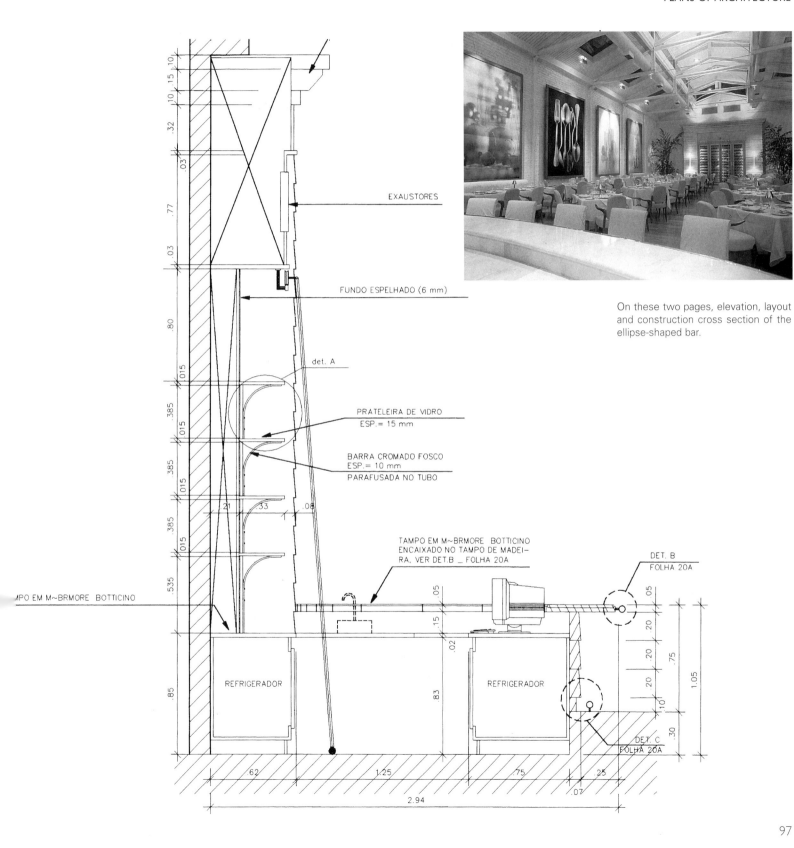

EXAUSTORES

FUNDO ESPELHADO (6 mm)

det. A

PRATELEIRA DE VIDRO
ESP.= 15 mm

BARRA CROMADO FOSCO
ESP.= 10 mm
PARAFUSADA NO TUBO

TAMPO EM M~BRMORE BOTTICINO
ENCAIXADO NO TAMPO DE MADEI-
RA, VER DET.B _ FOLHA 20A

MPO EM M~BRMORE BOTTICINO

REFRIGERADOR

REFRIGERADOR

DET. B
FOLHA 20A

DET. C
FOLHA 20A

On these two pages, elevation, layout
and construction cross section of the
ellipse-shaped bar.

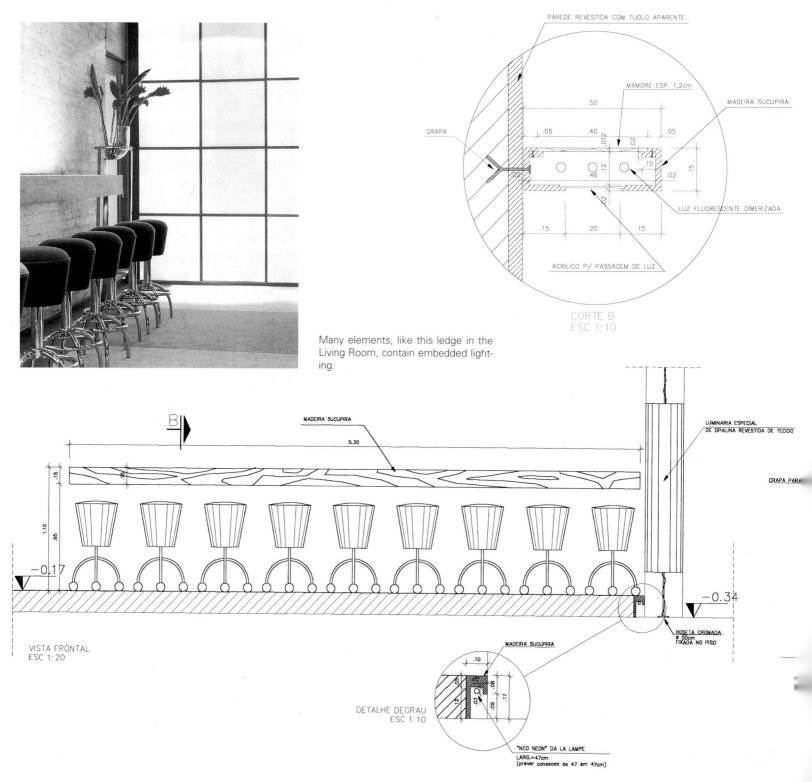

Many elements, like this ledge in the Living Room, contain embedded lighting.

PAREDE REVESTIDA COM TIJOLO APARENTE

MAMORE ESP. 1,2cm

MADEIRA SUCUPIRA

GRAPA

.50

.05   .40

.012   .02

.05

.02

.46   .12

.10

.15

.02

.15   .20   .15

LUZ FLUORESCENTE DIMERIZADA

ACRILICO P/ PASSAGEM DE LUZ

CORTE B
ESC 1:10

MADEIRA SUCUPIRA

LUMINARIA ESPECIAL
DE OPALINA REVESTIDA DE TECIDO

5.30

B

.15

GRAPA PARA

1.10

.95

−0.17

−0.34

ROSETA CROMADA
Ø 50cm
FIXADA NO PISO

VISTA FRONTAL
ESC 1:20

MADEIRA SUCUPIRA

.10

.08

.12   .17

.09

DETALHE DEGRAU
ESC 1:10

"NEO NEON" DA LA LAMPE

LARG.=47cm
(prever conexoes de 47 em 47cm)

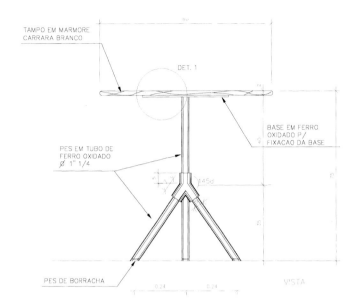

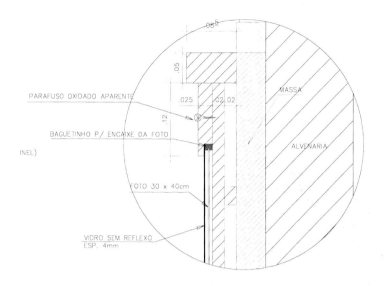

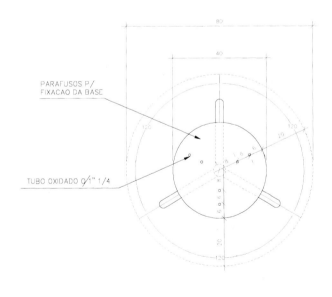

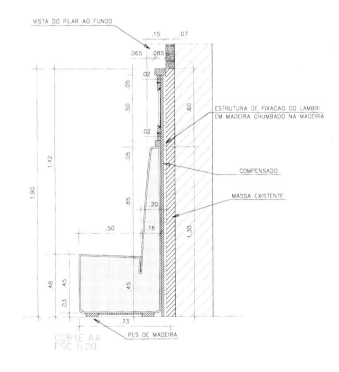

Construction plan of the tables in the
Living Room.

Construction plan of the sofas in the
Living Room.

Nobu
Location: *105 Hudson Street, New York, United States.*
Design: *David Rockwell, Chris Smith, Andrew Fuston.*
Year of opening: *1994.*
Client:*Drew Nieporent, Nobu Matsuhisa, Robert De Niro.*
Lighting: *Paul Gregory, Focus Lighting Inc.*
Trees: *John A. Savitieri Furniture.*
Chairs: *Thonet.*
Floor and curtains: *Julie Lifton-Schwerner.*
Plaster: *Visions in Plaster.*

Pâtisserie and Bistro Payard
Location: *1032 Lexington Avenue, New York, United States.*
Design: *David Rockwell.*
Year of opening: *1997.*
Client: *François Payard, Daniel Boulud.*
Kitchen design:*Patrick Vercysse.*

Mohegan Sun Casino
Location: *Uncasville, Connecticut, Estados Unidos.*
Design: *David Rockwell, Jay Valgora, Paul Vega, David Fritzinger.*
Interior design: *Suzanne Couture.*
Interior design team:*Masako Fukuoka, Linda Laucirica, Julia Roth,*
Eve-Lynn Schoenstein, Jeanne Valdez, Alice Yiu.
Executive architect:*Brennan Beer Gorman/Architects.*
Tribal adviser: *Mohegan Tribe of Indians.*
Structure: *DeSimone, Chaplin & Dobryn.*
Lighting: *Focus Lighting, Inc.*
Landscaping: *EDSA.*
Installations: *Lehr Associates.*

In establishments dedicated to leisure, architecture over the last years has tended to form part of the entertainment. It is not merely important to offer a service, but also to create some fiction, to stimulate the fantasy of the client and, in short, to create an attractive, imaginative and theatrical atmosphere.

David Rockwell is without doubt one of the architects who has worked most in the field of specialised entertaining architecture for restaurants. David Rockwell is responsible for the restaurants of the Planet Hollywood chain all over the world, the Official All Star Café in the United States, restaurants as well known as the Monkey Bar, the Torre de Pisa and the restaurants presented in this article: Nobu, Pâtisserie Payard and Mohegan Sun Casino.

The following pages show evidence that the architecture of entertainment is based on another type of planimetry. The drawings and the plans of projects like Mohegan Sun Casino or the Nobu have more things in common with a cinema set than with typical architecture.

In a certain way, firstly, it is necessary to invent a story, to draw the story board, so that later you can start to work with these images, decode them and make a coherent whole. The final result tries to be as faithful to the initial image as possible. The project is created in the phase before its architectual development (this only establishes the technical solutions).

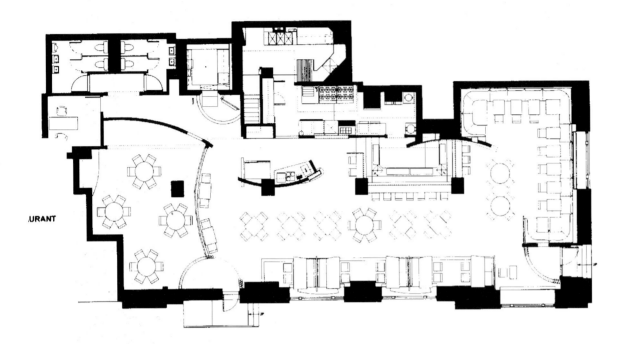

URANT

Although it is a Japanese restaurant, Nobu has little to do with the aesthetics of this kind of establishment. David Rockwell sought inspiration in rural Japan, where the chef Nobuyuki Matsuhisa was born. Most of the decor is related to plants, the most eye catching motif being a series of tree pillars built from birch trunks and sheets of rusted steel that serve as lighting elements. Elsewhere in the restaurant, rough, rustic finishes abound: a wall built from Japanese river pebbles, another from hand made tiles, beech wood flooring, a velvet curtain, blue papered walls with golden polka dots, etc.

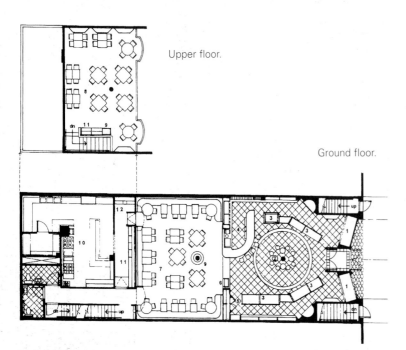

Upper floor.

Ground floor.

La Pâtisserie and Bistro Payard is an establishment that combines a pâtisserie, a bar and a restaurant in one. All these different activities mean that the premises are bustling all day: you can have breakfast, dinner, or just have a coffee and croissant at midday. The owners have declared that their intention is to make it a meeting point for all the neighbourhood.

The wood surfaces and the ochre and red tones stand out the most. The establishment is divided into various sectors. As soon as you cross the entrance a counter of pastries and cakes allows you to select from the varied offer of Payard. A second, more homely, space, the Bistro, is situated behind some wooden shelves. At the rear of the premises is the kitchen, while up above an attic has been converted into a tea room, with a splendid metal banister. The most characteristic element of the establishment are the art nouveau lamps designed by David Rockwell.

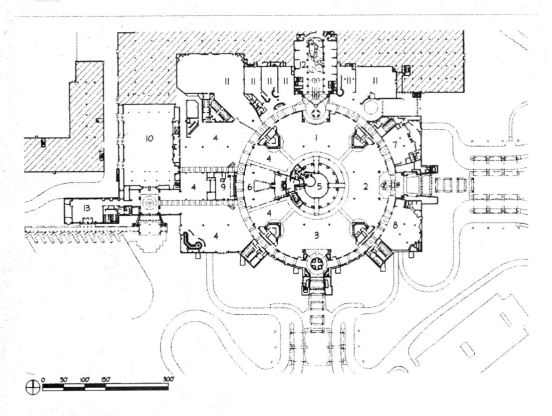

The Mohegan Sun Casino is on an Indian reserve of the Mohegan tribe between Norwich and Foxwoods. This encouraged the designers to incorporate Indian cultural elements into the project. The scheme includes a bingo-hall, a casino, and a bar-restaurant.

David Rockwell approached the projects through watercolors that show images full of color and people moving.